"With Shannon Kolakowski's empathic guidance you will learn to accept and love yourself—including your anxiety and shyness. Furthermore, you will develop new skills that will help you find love. If you are shy or socially anxious and want a loving relationship this is the book for you."

—**Michelle Skeen, PsyD**, author of *Love Me Don't Leave Me*

"Dating is a process of deliberate exploration. At one level we are exploring human relationships, but at another level dating opens us up to the world within. It opens us up to our hopes, aspirations, and values, but it also opens us up to our fears, anxieties, and judgments.

In the normal mode of mind we often suppose that the difficult material in that second territory is merely something to be gotten rid of so we can get back to dating. This book takes a much different approach: that territory is worthy of attention and exploration. It is part of the very fabric of our emotional lives that we bring to relationships themselves. If you are interested in exploring human relationships, consider the possibility that you have a much larger territory to explore as part of that very process. This gentle and wise book will show you how."

—**Steven C. Hayes, PhD**, Foundation Professor and Director of Clinical Training at the University of Nevada and author of *Get Out of Your Mind and Into Your Life*

"Shannon Kolakowski's book will be the first book I recommend to people who are single, shy, and looking for love. She really understands the fears of socially anxious people and how terrifying dating can be for them. Each chapter is filled with illustrative stories, questionnaires, and exercises that bring readers to a compassionate view of their dating fears and concerns and arms them with everything they need to start the dating process. It was a pleasure reviewing Kolakowski's new book. She is a very talented psychologist and a great writer."

—**Deborah Khoshaba, PsyD**, clinical psychologist specializing in resilience, personal growth, and health; director of program development and training for the Hardiness Institute; author of several books on the hardiness approach to stress management and resilience; founder of the popular blog *Psychology in Everyday Life*; and writer for psychologytoday.com

"Take charge of your dating life. *Single, Shy, and Looking for Love* explains, in easy-to-understand language, how to approach shyness and social anxiety from a new and empowering perspective. Learn how to build the skills and confidence essential to dating success. Get ready to take those important first steps toward finding love."

—**Leah Klungness, Ph.D**, psychologist and coauthor of *The Complete Single Mother*

"In *Single, Shy, and Looking for Love*, psychologist Shannon Kolakowski offers a thoughtful, evidence-based, readable, and practical book for those seeking love and partnered relationships who tend to be anxious and shy. She effectively uses best practices and the latest thinking about anxiety management to help those who are looking for love. Her book is full of practical suggestions, exercises, and wisdom to help those who may struggle with dating and finding the right mate. Kudos to Kolakowski for an excellent book that is bound to help many."

> —**Thomas Plante, PhD, ABPP**, Augustin Cardinal Bea, S.J. University Professor, director of the Spirituality and Health Institute at Santa Clara University, and author of *Religion, Spirituality, and Positive Psychology: Understanding the Psychological Fruits of Faith, Sexual Abuse in the Catholic Church: A Decade of Crisis, 2002-2012,* and *Spiritual Practices in Psychotherapy: Thirteen Tools for Enhancing Psychological Health*

"Shannon Kolakowski demonstrates that there's no need to feel powerless in dating. *Single, Shy, and Looking for Love* will help both women and men identify the source of dating anxiety, and it offers real strategies for getting out there and finding love. This excellent book contains powerful techniques for mastering shyness and focusing instead on dating strategies that work. If anxiety is keeping you from finding the love of your life, please read this book. It might just change your life."

> —**Shawn T. Smith, PsyD**, clinical psychologist and author of *The User's Guide to the Human Mind* and *The Woman's Guide to How Men Think*

SINGLE, SHY,

AND LOOKING FOR

LOVE

A Dating Guide for the
Shy & Socially Anxious

Shannon Kolakowski, PsyD

New Harbinger Publications, Inc.

"Finding the Sweet Spot" and "Heightening the Sweet Spot" adapted from chapter 6, "Mindfulness, Values, and Therapeutic Relationship in Acceptance and Commitment Therapy" by Kelly G. Wilson and Emily K. Sandoz, in MINDFULNESS AND THE THERAPEUTIC RELATIONSHIP, edited by Steven F. Hick and Thomas Bien and copyright © 2008 The Guilford Press. Used by permission of The Guilford Press; permission conveyed through Copyright Clearance Center, Inc.

Distributed in Canada by Raincoast Books

Copyright © 2014 by Shannon Kolakowski
          New Harbinger Publications, Inc.
          5674 Shattuck Avenue
          Oakland, CA 94609
          www.newharbinger.com

Cover design by Amy Shoup
Text design by Michele Waters-Kermes
Acquired by Melissa Kirk
Edited by Jasmine Star

Library of Congress Cataloging-in-Publication Data on file

Printed in the United States of America

16   15   14

10   9   8   7   6   5   4   3   2   1   First printing

I dedicate this book to my husband, Rob.

Contents

Acknowledgments

I loved writing this book and am deeply thankful to those who helped it become a reality. Many thanks to Melissa Kirk, Jess Beebe, Nicola Skidmore, Amy Shoup, Adia Colar, Bevin Donahue, Rachel Dinkin, Vicraj Gill, Michele Waters, Lisa Gunther, and the entire team at New Harbinger. I am lucky to have had such an insightful, supportive group by my side.

I am grateful to my clients. Thank you for sharing your lives with me and for allowing me to be a part of your journey toward love. I'm so glad to have known each and every one of you. Thanks also to the readers who have contacted me. Your feedback, stories, and comments help me stay motivated and feel connected, so thank you for reaching out to me. I love hearing from you!

I'm thankful to my husband, who made our first date a delight and a pleasure, and who calmed my nerves with his warmth, humor, and charm—and by being a genuinely honest, good guy. Without you, I wouldn't understand what all the fuss about love is about and why the agony of dating is so worthwhile in the end. You're truly and simply my favorite person and I love you, always.

Introduction

Love isn't designed just for certain people. It has nothing to do with any magical way of approaching women, making sure the guy makes all the first moves, or being the most attractive or wealthy person. It's not about forcing yourself to be bubbly and outgoing, or trying to be someone you're not. You could drive yourself crazy trying to follow all the rules set forth by dating gurus. Those guidelines tend to perpetuate the idea that you need to be on guard, monitoring what you do and say during dating situations, in order to find love. If you're shy or anxious, you're already painfully aware of what you're doing in the presence of someone you like. Trying to act or behave in certain ways as you walk on eggshells trying to control, squash, ignore, or threaten your anxiety into submission isn't going to work.

What if finding love isn't about having to work against who you are and what you fear? What if you could learn to be okay with some of your anxiety while still pursuing the love life you want? What if the answer lies in being less worried about being embarrassed and less concerned with how your love interest judges you? Imagine if, instead of worrying about what you'll say the next time you come face-to-face with an attractive person, you could feel confident in your ability to interact and be okay with how it goes, come what may.

Let me suggest that the reason you haven't found love (yet!) is that your relationship with your anxiety has been a roadblock to being able to listen to and act on your innermost feelings, goals, values, and desires. What if your reaction to your anxiety is causing you to act in ways that are contrary to what you really want from life? What if your worry about your anxiety has stopped you from discovering or connecting with what you really want in a relationship?

When Social Anxiety Begins

I've seen shyness and anxiety affect all stages of dating, mating, and falling in love. Your level of anxiety may be so great that the very idea of approaching a potential date or being approached by someone causes you to shut down. Because of your anxiety, perhaps you've never been on a date or have had very little experience in dating. You may feel lonely and discouraged and wonder why you can't find what so many others have. And if you've spent a long time feeling frustrated, disappointed, and isolated, you may have begun to wonder if it will ever happen for you.

On the other hand, you may be able to get to the point of initiating or accepting a date, whether through an online dating site or in person, but struggle with being yourself on dates, knowing what to say (or not to say), or being painfully aware of how the other person might be evaluating you. Or perhaps you can get through one or two dates fairly easily but then have trouble after the initial phase of "getting acquainted" as the idea of developing a relationship or becoming sexually intimate causes your anxiety to kick into overdrive. And if you survive the early stage of getting to know someone well, you may continue to struggle with insecurity and find yourself withdrawing or becoming more anxious when the relationship hits a rough patch.

You may also be considering reentering the dating scene after a divorce or the end of a long-term relationship. Years of not dating may have left you feeling unprepared and anxious about the prospect of dating again. You may struggle with feeling overwhelmed, vulnerable, jaded, or uncertain and want guidance in how you can feel more comfortable about dating.

What all of these situations have in common is the fear of feeling anxious or embarrassed in the presence of someone you're interested in. But it doesn't have to be that way. This book is designed to help you approach your thoughts and feelings about dating in a whole new way. Rather than being driven by anxiety and fear, you'll learn to make choices based on living the life you want with the kind of people you want to have in it. By learning to bring objective awareness, compassion, and a sense of nonattachment to rigid beliefs about dating, you can create space in your life to take actions in line with what you really want. Rather than letting anxiety and shyness hold you back from dating, you'll begin to interact with and date people you're attracted to.

Whether your anxiety stems from the idea of hanging out with someone you're interested in at a party, going on a one-on-one date for coffee, reentering the dating scene, or knowing how to approach the sexual aspects of dating, this book will help you end your struggle with dating anxiety. It addresses the most common ways people get stuck or feel helpless in their dating life. Whether it's getting caught up in your thoughts or emotions, not knowing what you want, having habits of withdrawal or hurtful action, or confining yourself to certain roles, this book can help.

Getting Unstuck Through Acceptance and Commitment Therapy

Acceptance and commitment therapy (ACT; pronounced as the word "act") takes a new approach to treating anxiety and has been proven effective for social anxiety (Dalrymple and Herbert 2007). In the ACT approach, you're encouraged to stop trying to cope with your fears around dating; instead, you allow the fears to be and simply see them as thoughts, sensations, or painful feelings that will come and go. Rather than basing your actions on avoiding feeling anxious or embarrassed, you can learn to notice your worried thoughts without acting on what they tell you to do. ACT helps you see that you don't have to be ruled by your anxiety; it doesn't have to dictate your life.

Anxiety, and specifically social anxiety, tends to make it difficult to focus on the bigger picture in life. There's a hyperfocus on small interactions and just getting through the anxiety-provoking situations you encounter. But ACT offers an alternative, creating an opportunity to live well and with intention, noticing the larger meaning and value in your life. As you begin to live each day as if it were a precious gift, you may view things that had seemed very important from a new perspective, and have a greater connection to the vital essence of being alive.

The exercises in this book are structured around the six core processes of ACT as they apply to dating anxiety and shyness. Those processes are acceptance, being present, cognitive defusion, self-as-context, values clarification, and committed action (Hayes, Strosahl, and Wilson 1999):

- → *Acceptance* has to do with approaching your anxiety in a new way. It's about embracing experiences rather than avoiding them.

- → *Being present* is about showing up in the moment and being aware of the here and now.

- → *Cognitive defusion* is about seeing how your thoughts affect your behavior, including around dating, and developing a new relationship to your thoughts.

- → *Self-as-context* has to do with figuring out how your self-concept affects your coping style and breaking free of past constraints so you can choose to be comfortable in your own skin.

- → *Values clarification* helps you figure out what you really want from life and love.

- → *Committed action* helps you get there.

The phrase "accept, choose, and take action" is a simplified way of thinking about what ACT encourages you to do. ACT will help you move past your dating fears, discover what you really want in a relationship, and take steps toward getting what you want.

Accept

A large part of the human experience is wishing things were different than they are. Given that you're single and reading this book, you probably wish you'd meet a partner who's loving, attractive, and caring, and who wants to be in a committed relationship with you. You probably wish your anxiety wasn't holding you back from meeting someone or pursuing someone you met at the coffee shop. You may think, *If only I were better looking or had more money, I'd attract the right kind of person.* Amidst all of that hoping and wishing for things to be different, your energy and time are sucked into a vortex of struggle.

Acceptance, one of the core components of ACT, means acknowledging the reality of your current situation with a nonjudgmental and understanding attitude. Rather than wishing you weren't shy or anxious, you learn to accept that you will probably always experience some degree of anxiety, but that it doesn't have to dictate your actions. Falling in love will undoubtedly cause increased anxiety at times, but you can learn to tolerate some anxiety in order to pursue the love life you value. This also opens you up to experiencing the other feelings that come with falling in love: excitement, wonder, intimacy, and connection.

Choose

In order to fall in love, you need to be able to connect with the present moment. Think about a time when you had a conversation with someone who didn't seem to be completely there. Maybe the other person was preoccupied or seemed uninterested. It made it hard to connect, didn't it?

The antidote is mindfulness: keeping your attention on the here and now, rather than thinking about past dating mistakes, planning ways to avoid things that might go wrong in future dating scenarios, or dreading the possibility of living a lifetime of loneliness. This crucial component of ACT requires an open, curious, and nonjudgmental perspective. Throughout the book, I'll offer exercises and techniques for practicing mindfulness and acceptance and help you see how these skills can improve your dating and love life.

As you learn to stay in the present moment and let go of wishing things were different than they are, your suffering due to anxiety will decrease. And as your suffering decreases, you'll have more room to begin making choices and changes that reflect what you want to do differently.

This is where the next component of ACT—choose—really comes into play: choosing what matters to you in life and the kind of person you want to be, and letting go of ideas about yourself that may have held you back before. So often, we get stuck in a role and feel helpless to change who we think we are: *I'm super shy. I guess I'm just not meant for love. I've always had trouble with girls. I'm not the kind of girl that guys ask out.* When you make these kinds of statements about yourself and believe them, they start to define your role in the world. You may have come to believe that your destiny or role in life is to be lonely or have limited options when it comes to dating. The approach in this book will help you open the door to a new world of possibilities. You'll learn to redefine and expand your identity and begin to live a life that's more in line with your true self. You'll learn to fearlessly examine yourself and the life you want to lead while choosing to pursue relationships that reflect those values.

Take Action

When you have a goal in mind, the way to achieve it is usually to start doing some things differently. If you've been paralyzed by anxiety, the committed action steps in this book will clearly show you what to do differently to start meeting people, dating, and developing relationships.

Committed action is about being willing and prepared to try new behaviors and ways of thinking. It helps you get out from under worry and start moving in desired directions. Along the way, I'll offer guidance on how to increase your confidence, be romantic, be more engaged in conversations, and make others feels special. I'll also address how to be available without being needy and how to set boundaries without playing games. You'll learn how to choose people who are compatible with you and how to let go of those who aren't.

In these pages, your most pressing dating questions are addressed, help to you define what committed action looks like for you:

- *How and where do I find potential mates?*
- *What are effective ways to initiate contact with others?*
- *How do I handle insecurities about my appearance?*
- *How do I respond to dating requests?*
- *Rather than retreat or avoid someone I like, how can I show I'm interested?*
- *How do I know if I've found the right partner?*
- *How and when do I bring up commitment or taking it to the next level?*
- *How do I handle worries or fears surrounding sex?*
- *How much should I share about myself when dating?*
- *What's the best way to handle awkward dating situations?*
- *How do I deal with rejection and unreciprocated feelings?*
- *How do I handle my anxieties about starting a new relationship?*

- *What relationship skills do I need to develop to help love last?*

Toward the end of the book, you'll also learn skills and techniques for when you're ready to move from dating to beginning a committed relationship. The tools and skills of ACT can help you solidify your relationship, deal with anxiety issues as they arise, and build a meaningful relationship together. Here's a glimpse at what you'll learn:

- How to increase intimacy and closeness in a relationship
- How to deal with shyness and performance anxiety in the bedroom
- How and when to use validation and how to get it
- How to accept your partner for who he is and how to resist the urge to change him
- How to communicate assertively and share in a constructive way

Throughout, the goal is not to try to control or get rid of your anxiety; rather, the goal is to learn to experience your anxiety fully in the service of living a valued life, complete with the entire range of emotions that will arise along the way. Using your larger goals in life as a motivator, ACT will help you approach and even embrace feared experiences.

ACT has been proven to work for people just like you. Outcome studies have shown that ACT results in significant reductions in avoidance (Dalrymple and Herbert 2007), as well as reductions in anxiety, worry thoughts, and depression, along with increases in mindfulness and acceptance (Kocovski, Fleming, and Rector 2009). While some of the strategies I present may initially feel counterintuitive, I invite you to be open to them. Try the exercises for yourself and pay attention to how it feels to do things in new ways. With time, you'll discover for yourself how powerful these techniques are.

Who This Book Is For

This book is for women and men of all ages who have trouble finding or maintaining a relationship because of dating and relationship anxiety. Whether you've never had a relationship or are divorced and having anxiety about reentering the dating scene, this book is for you. The concepts discussed are geared toward people who have difficulty with social situations across a variety of settings and are particularly fearful of dating. But the strategies will work for anyone who has ever had any level of anxiety or shyness around dating. In each chapter, I'll give you case examples from people I've worked with who've used these tools to overcome their anxiety and thrive.

Throughout the book, I alternate between referring to a potential partner as "he" or "she," as this book is written for both women and men. Most of the scenarios apply to everyone. In the instances where gender does make a difference, I'll address how gender may play a role.

How to Use This Book

This book is different than other dating guides you may have encountered. It provides practical advice about dating and anxiety, but it also helps you examine your relationship with yourself. It doesn't just tell you what to do; it helps you figure out what you want to do and why. It doesn't just assume you'll get over tough emotions; it tells you how to handle the thoughts and feelings that accompany stepping out of your comfort zone.

This book will serve you best if you read it sequentially and take the time to complete or practice all of the exercises. These pages offer you the potential to make a new beginning—one filled with the very real likelihood that you'll find love. You'll discover that learning to accept all aspects of yourself, even your anxiety and shyness, while trying out new ways of interacting with others, will help you find love.

CHAPTER 1

Understanding Why You're So Nervous

A client of mine, Andrew, came to me as a graduate student in his final year of law school. He'd had one girlfriend briefly during his freshman year of college, and he'd shared his first and only sexual experience with her. Since then, he'd just been on three or four dates, and he told me that he'd found the dates to be extremely uncomfortable and awkward. While he tended to be friends with many women, he was hesitant to initiate romantic relationships with women he was interested in. On a few occasions, he'd asked out girls who hadn't been receptive. Hearing them say no crushed his confidence and made it harder for him to get past his shy reserve.

Andrew started his law school internship at a local courthouse in the spring. Another intern was a young woman named Cara, who had long dark hair and a friendly smile. Andrew liked her intelligence and thought she was pretty. He was immediately attracted to her, and as he got to know her, it became clear to him that she was interested in him too. So he gathered up his courage and asked her to have lunch with him the next Friday. When she said yes, his joy at her acceptance quickly was replaced by dread.

As the day of the date approached, Andrew became consumed with self-doubt and nerves. What would he talk about? How could he show Cara that he liked her without being overly enthusiastic? What if he started saying ridiculous things and embarrassed himself? Thinking about all of the ways their lunch could go wrong was terrifying and overwhelming, and Andrew started to believe it was entirely possible—in fact probable—that Cara would leave the date thinking he was completely strange and pathetic, and that he would never live down his shame. His anxiety became so great that he finally made up an excuse to get out of the date. He stopped talking to Cara much at work because he was ashamed of the way he'd acted, and eventually he gave up on the idea of dating her.

Andrew's fear about how his anxiety could potentially affect the date got in the way of following his heart and taking a chance. His beliefs about how wrong things could go or how bad it would feel prevented him from potentially finding a connection with Cara.

❣

The truth is, dating is a bit intimidating for most people. But if you're shy or socially anxious, it's more than intimidating; it can be downright painful and terrifying. You may monitor every move you make, and your worry about being judged or found lacking may only worsen as you try to do or say the right thing, wanting desperately to avoid embarrassing yourself. Yet often, the harder you try, the less you feel like yourself. You probably want to retreat, hide, or do anything possible to get away from the awkwardness you feel. Like Andrew, you may end up feeling like it's better to be safe and alone than to risk being hurt.

Fortunately, all of that can change, and this book will show you the way. But in order to learn new ways of approaching dating, it's essential to first understand shyness, social anxiety, and anxiety disorders and see how they can affect dating and relationships.

Shyness

If you consider yourself a shy person, it's likely that you tend to be uncomfortable, quiet, and reserved in social situations, especially when you're meeting someone new or talking to a potential love interest. With shyness, you may feel as though you'd like to have close relationships with others, but it seems too difficult to meet people, or you can't imagine maintaining a long-term relationship with anyone new (Roisman et al. 2004). There's often a sense of loneliness (Mounts et al. 2006) and isolation (Schmidt and Fox 1995). Indeed, research shows that young adults who are shy tend to date less than their nonshy peers (Leck 2006) and aren't as likely to be in a committed or high-quality relationship (Nelson et al. 2008).

The most common symptoms of shyness include the following (Sieber and Meyers 1992):

→ Feeing tense, self-conscious, and awkward around others

→ Being uneasy in social situations

→ Having discomfort in unfamiliar settings

→ Fearing or avoiding group settings, such as parties or social events

→ Thinking carefully and persisting in problem solving

→ Questioning your abilities or having trouble with self-confidence

→ Feeling less in control of your own fate

Clearly, shyness can have a big effect on dating. Dating is a process that involves meeting someone new, getting to know the person, and deciding whether this is someone you're attracted to and want to spend time with. You have to figure out whether the two of you have common interests and share similar values and goals. A certain amount of judgment and evaluation is required to determine whether a person is someone you want to see again, someone you want to date but perhaps not be in a serious relationship with, or someone you might want to develop a deeper relationship with. In this way, both you and your date are evaluating your potential compatibility. But when you're shy, this aspect of evaluation and being judged can be too painful to bear. Shy people tend to be hyperaware of and sensitive to how others might view them. Therefore, the process of dating brings up uncomfortable emotions and upsetting thoughts.

On the other hand, the thought of having to potentially let down someone who's interested in you when you don't feel the same way may seem unbearable. You may wonder, *How can I hurt someone's feelings that way? What am I supposed to say?* Dealing with rejection—either receiving it or giving it—is never easy, but you'll become more comfortable with it as you progress through this book.

People who are shy have a higher likelihood of having social anxiety, and many of the traits overlap. But being shy doesn't mean you automatically have social anxiety disorder. In fact, about 82 percent of people who are shy do not have social anxiety disorder (Heiser, Turner, and Beidel 2003).

Social Anxiety Disorder

Social anxiety disorder (SAD) affects 7 to 12 percent of the population (Kessler et al. 2005) and is the third-most-common psychological disorder in the United States (Kashdan and Herbert 2001). SAD is defined as the "persistent fear of one or more situations in which the person is exposed to possible scrutiny by others and fears that he or she may do something or act in a way that will be humiliating or embarrassing" (American Psychiatric Association 2013, 241).

With SAD, your anxiety may occur when you have to meet new people or are in a group setting and feel you are being judged or evaluated by others. You may worry that you'll be embarrassed or humiliated by visible symptoms of anxiety. You may have physical symptoms such as blushing, sweating, rapid heart rate, quavering voice, or shakiness, or you may have no outwardly apparent symptoms. Either way, because of your fear, you end up avoiding social settings and may find even the thought of going into a new social situation upsetting.

Social anxiety is a chronic problem, affecting people for an average duration of 22.9 years (Wittchen et al. 2000). Because of its long span, social anxiety can have long-standing effects on quality of life if left untreated. It can affect your work performance, prevent you from developing friendships, and hurt your ability to successfully date and find romantic partners.

The *Diagnostic and Statistical Manual of Mental Disorders* (American Psychiatric Association 2013), the manual that psychologists, psychiatrists, and doctors use to diagnose psychological disorders, defines social anxiety disorder as having the following symptoms:

→ You have marked fear or anxiety about one or more social situations in which you feel exposed to possible scrutiny by others, such as having a conversation, eating or drinking with others, or giving a speech.

→ You fear that you'll show anxiety symptoms or act in a way that will offend others or be negatively evaluated by them, causing you to feel humiliated, embarrassed, or rejected.

→ You either actively avoid these social situations or endure them with marked fear or anxiety.

→ You recognize that your fear or anxiety is out of proportion to the actual threat posed by the social situation.

→ Your fear, anxiety, or avoidance of these social situations lasts six months or longer.

→ Your level of fear, anxiety, and avoidance causes significant distress or impairment in your social life, work life, or other important areas of your daily life.

Social anxiety has an early age of onset, meaning its symptoms are likely to first appear during childhood, or in the early teen years, between ages fourteen and seventeen (Stein and Gorman 2001). If you have social anxiety, in childhood you may have been worried about being separated from your parents, had an upset stomach or stomachache when nervous, or had trouble going to school in the mornings because of feelings of fear or nervousness. You may have feared that something awful would happen to a family member, feared being in crowded places like a busy playground or cafeteria, felt nervous if you had to stay away from home overnight, or felt scared of the dark. Because of your hesitation in social situations, you may have had less opportunity to form close relationships and experience positive social support, which would have added to your feelings of isolation and loneliness. In addition, those who have teen-onset social anxiety can often recall a specific social incident that was embarrassing or acutely stressful that occurred prior to developing SAD (Rosellini et al. 2013).

Social anxiety also clearly affects relationships in adulthood. Adults who are socially anxious tend to be less emotionally expressive, be less open in sharing or talking about themselves, and have lower levels of intimacy in romantic relationships (Sparrevohn and Rapee 2009). They also have a tendency to express more negativity when sharing their feelings and experiences with their partners (Wenzel et al. 2005), which can lead to less closeness in their relationships (Kashdan et al. 2007).

Because of their difficulties in forming and keeping close relationships, people with social anxiety are less likely to date and marry than those with other forms of anxiety disorders (Wittchen et al. 2000). And finally, if you're single and have SAD, you're more likely than someone who's married to avoid social situations and to have a mood disorder. Ultimately, the more severe social anxiety is, the more likely it is to affect your ability to form strong relationships (Hart et al. 1999).

Many people have some of the symptoms of SAD but don't quality for a full diagnosis of social anxiety disorder. In some ways, SAD is like a continuum, with high social anxiety on one end and only moderate social anxiety on the other. You probably fluctuate in where you fall on the scale depending on the circumstances and how stressed you are in other areas of your life. Regardless of where you are on the spectrum, the tools and techniques in this book will help you change your relationship to your anxiety and open up in intimate relationships.

Panic Attacks and Panic Disorder

You may have developed *panic attacks* that occur when you're faced with the prospect of a new dating situation or being in a new group of people. During a panic attack, you may experience shortness of breath, a lump in your throat, rapid heartbeat, dizziness, nausea, flushing of your face, tingling in your hands or feet, muscle weakness, a sensation of shakiness, light-headedness, ringing in your ears, or hyperventilation. You may worry that you're losing control or going crazy or even fear that you're going to die, although these symptoms aren't actually lethal. Because the panic is so unpleasant, you may end up adjusting your routine and avoiding certain places or activities to reduce your chance of having a panic attack. If panic attacks occur repeatedly, you may develop *panic disorder*, which is marked by fear of having a panic attack and not being able to escape or get help.

If you have panic attacks, one of the reasons you experience higher levels of physiological arousal when you're anxious—like blushing, sweating, or rapid heartbeat—could be a phenomenon called *anxiety sensitivity* (Reiss and McNally 1985). People who have anxiety sensitivity are much more attuned to bodily sensations such as rapid heartbeat, and tend to have a heightened response to stress.

Therefore, when you feel stressed about being on a date, you're more likely to notice that you have elevated heartbeat and breathing rates, both symptoms of anxiety. As you focus on your body's sensations, you begin to interpret them as signals that something is very wrong with you, perhaps believing that you're having a heart attack or nervous breakdown. In this way, your response to your anxiety symptoms causes you to feel out of control and in danger (McNally 1989). Ignoring your anxiety symptoms feels impossible because your anxiety sensitivity causes you to focus on your physiological sensations and closely monitor your body for signs of danger. The result is a vicious cycle of hypervigilance and fear of how anxiety will affect your body, leading to heightened symptoms, and on and on.

The antidote to this cycle, which we'll explore in upcoming chapters, is to change the way you respond to your anxiety symptoms. Rather than seeing panic as your enemy, you can learn to see your symptoms for what they are (anxiety) and accept them as a nonharmful (albeit uncomfortable) part of your anxiety. As you move away from trying to monitor, prevent, or decrease your symptoms, you'll notice that they become less intense and shorter in duration.

Generalized Anxiety Disorder

Generalized anxiety disorder (GAD) is a condition that involves anxiety about a number of events and activities across a broad spectrum, rather than worrying about a more specific event or social situations. With GAD, you feel perpetually anxious or overwhelmed by everyday things, like school or work responsibilities, and your anxiety becomes higher during periods of high stress. You worry about many aspects of your future and may fear that you're doomed. No matter how hard you try to let things go, you feel like you can't stop worrying. If you have GAD, it's likely that you feel you've been a worrier for your entire life—so much so that your level of worry almost feels normal. However, ongoing high levels of anxiety interfere with your quality of life, and your responses to stress take a toll on your well-being.

Physical symptoms of GAD include the following:

→ Long-standing feelings of restlessness

→ Ongoing tension

→ A feeling of being on edge

→ Irritability

→ Difficulty concentrating

→ Sleep problems

→ Ongoing muscle tension

→ Stomach pain

→ Joint, neck, or back pain

In order to be diagnosed with GAD, your anxiety must persist for at least six months and cause you significant distress or interfere with your daily life. GAD is the most common form of anxiety disorder and is often accompanied by depression.

Ruling Out Medical Explanations

Because the physical symptoms of anxiety and panic attacks can be similar to symptoms of medical conditions, such as thyroid problems, heart conditions, and vertigo, it's important to see your primary care physician in order to rule out any physical cause of these symptoms. Once a medical cause has been ruled out, you can move forward knowing that your physical symptoms truly are a manifestation of anxiety sensitivity and not a signal that your body needs medical treatment.

Depression

Depression affects a person's moods, thoughts, and behaviors through a sense of pervasive sadness, emptiness, numbness, or loss of interest in previously enjoyed activities. If you have an anxiety disorder, there's a good chance you'll also have problems with depression. Depression and anxiety are so frequently seen together that many researchers believe it's actually more likely for people to experience both, as opposed to only depression (Rapaport 2001). With mixed depression and anxiety, you'll notice that you tend to expect the worst, feel hopeless about the future, have feelings of worthlessness, have difficulty concentrating, have trouble sleeping, have low energy, have high irritability and worry, and move through your day with a sense of hypervigilance, or constantly feeling on guard (Rivas-Vazquez et al. 2004).

One way that depression affects dating is by putting a damper on motivation to go on dates or interact with others in a social way; it makes you more likely to withdraw and seek isolation. Depression can also lower your sex drive and inhibit sexual desire, which may lead to problems as a new relationship progresses and becomes more intimate. Lastly, depression can affect dating by creating self-doubt and feelings of low self-worth, leading you to feel unworthy or undeserving of someone you'd otherwise be interested in. These are frequent problems for anxious daters, and I'll address them throughout the book.

Alcohol Use

Alcohol use is also often related to problems with anxiety. One study found that 23.3 percent of people who suffer from social anxiety disorder also suffer from an alcohol use disorder (Thomas, Thevos, and Randall 1999). This may happen because alcohol can help you feel more comfortable and competent in social situations (Thomas, Randall, and Carrigan 2003). When alcohol becomes a crutch you use to help you get through social events or dates, it can easily become a habit or abuse problem. Plus, being intoxicated on a date makes it hard to be yourself and get to know your partner. You're more likely to do or say things that are out of character, and this can get in the way of developing real intimacy. Therefore, moderation or abstaining from alcohol is key to working through your dating anxiety, rather than numbing it with drinks.

Dating Anxiety

The term *dating anxiety* refers to worry, distress, and inhibition experienced in social situations that involve dating partners or potential dating partners (Glickman and La Greca 2004). It affects people of all ages, ranging from adolescents to older adults reentering the dating world (Chorney and Morris 2008). With dating anxiety, the days leading up to a date or interaction can be grueling as you worry about what may go wrong, and the hours and days after a date are excruciating as you replay what happened over and over again.

Dating anxiety can impair your ability to develop relationships in many ways. One way it does so is by limiting your range of potential mates. The more people you have a chance to date and interact with, the greater your chances of finding someone really special. In this way, dating is a numbers game. Plus, if you're unable to meet or open up to many people, you may have less of an idea of what you're looking for in a partner or which traits are most compatible with yours.

Dating anxiety may also end up hurting your ability to connect with people you like. You're likely to experience a running critical commentary during dates, telling you things like *That was a stupid thing to say* or *Why would she be interested in that? You're being boring.* These self-critical thoughts leave you more on edge and less open, present, and genuine, making it difficult for your date to get to know you. Having this type of harsh perspective can also make you more critical and judgmental about potential partners. Being guarded or ruling someone out based on a small amount of information can sabotage your chances of giving a potentially good partner a fair chance.

In addition, dating anxiety can also cause people to stay in a relationship that's unfulfilling due to fear of having to date again if they break up with their partner. They do themselves a disservice, settling for a subpar relationship because anxiety rules their choices and limits their options.

Whatever your situation, this book will help you feel confident in a variety of dating situations and allow you to discover what you truly want in a relationship. The first step is to assess the extent to which anxiety is affecting your dating. The following quiz will help you do just that.

——→ Exercise: Assessing How Much Anxiety Is Affecting Your Dating

This quiz will help you take a closer look at how anxiety is contributing to your problems with dating. Read each statement below; then, on the line to the left of each, write the score that best indicates how this statement applies to you, using the following scale: 1 = rarely or never; 2 = sometimes; 3 = often; and 4 = very often. (You may also download this quiz at http://www.newharbinger.com/30031. See the back of this book for more details.)

_____ I fear that the person I go on a date with will find fault with me.

_____ On dates, I overuse or rely on alcohol to deal with my anxiety.

_____ I fear that I'm not good enough for the type of people I'd like to date.

_____ I worry about the repercussions of appearing aggressive, pushy, or desperate in dating situations.

_____ I feel nervous about approaching someone I'm attracted to.

_____ The prospect of initiating sexual activity makes me feel highly nervous.

_____ The idea of turning down a date's sexual advances makes me feel highly uncomfortable and worried.

_____ I feel anxious about my ability to find a potential date.

_____ I worry about how to manage my emotions about dating.

_____ The prospect of actively looking for someone to go on a date with causes anxiety.

_____ I often feel anxious when talking to someone I find attractive.

_____ I worry that I'll do or say something that will lead me to feel humiliated or embarrassed when I'm around someone I like.

_____ I worry that my date will judge my appearance in a negative way.

_____ The prospect of being rejected by someone I like leads to strong feelings of fear and worry.

_____ Calling a potential romantic partner causes me great apprehension.

_____ It takes me much longer to become comfortable around new people.

_____ I end up letting dating opportunities pass me by even though I wish I could respond in a more proactive or engaged way.

_____ I avoid going on dates.

If you answered 3 or 4 for at least four of the questions, it's likely that your anxiety is hurting your dating life. These scores indicate that dating doesn't just bring up everyday nerves or jitters; it brings out a heightened and debilitating sense of anxiety and self-consciousness. If you answered 1 or 2 for most of the statements, anxiety may not have significantly impaired your dating life. However, it will still be helpful to find new ways of approaching your anxiety and to get more in touch with what you want from a romantic partner. The techniques and practices in this book will be invaluable in deepening your capacity for self-compassion and acceptance and aiding in your journey toward love.

Coping Style

As you've seen, some of the most common worries about dating involve anxiety about rejection, fear of being embarrassed or humiliated, fear of not being good enough, fear of being judged, and worries about sexual intimacy. Other sources of dating worries include anxiety about feeling weak or broken, a need for control, fear of repeating negative experiences from the past, fear of emotional intimacy, and rumination, or not letting go of worry. In this section, we'll look at how these relationship fears develop and how the way you cope with these fears relates to your relationship success.

The way you interact with others and cope with conflict or potential ruptures in relationships is your relationship coping style. There are three primary coping styles, or ways of relating to others: moving away from others, moving toward others, and moving against others (Teyber and McClure 2011). Inflexible coping styles act as *defense mechanisms*—behaviors that increase your sense of safety when you feel hurt or attacked or have unmet needs.

People usually learn these coping styles in childhood, when they discover that a particular style of reacting to conflict or painful feelings works well in guarding against anxiety. If your parents weren't very involved with your life as you were growing up or if you were neglected, you may have learned to deal with problems on your own, allowing you to avoid the anxiety associated with needing others. The result is often a coping style of moving away from others. If your parents placed high expectations on you and rewarded you for behaving in ways that were beneficial to them, but criticized you when you didn't meet their needs, you may have learned to try to please others in order to avoid their disapproval. The result is often a coping style of moving toward others.

Coping styles can be problematic if they become overly rigid or inflexible. When you typically respond to others only in a certain way (moving toward, away from, or against), it can damage your ability to form and keep close relationships. As you read the following descriptions of each coping style, think about which style you tend to use.

Moving Away from Others

Whenever Brad found himself beginning to get into a serious relationship, he had a tendency to shut down emotionally. It always felt like the women he dated were too needy or emotionally involved. He often found himself backing away, especially if there was conflict or emotional turmoil. He generally didn't experience strong emotions, and he didn't know how to respond to girlfriends when they got upset. Usually, the more he withdrew, the more frustrated they'd get, causing him to want to retreat even more.

Brad's coping style is moving away from others. At an early age, he learned not to depend on others, and he prefers to be independent and autonomous. He has trouble showing affection and attending to the needs of the women he goes out with. Dating casually is comfortable for him, and he realizes that part of him feels incapable of having a long-term relationship.

Chloe also tends to move away from others, but only people she really likes. She's comfortable being open with her friends and guys she isn't attracted to, but she becomes guarded and extremely closed off whenever she's around someone she's attracted to. Those situations bring up fears of rejection and being judged as not good enough—fears that aren't activated around men she isn't attracted to. In response to her fear of judgment, she shuts down and is cold toward guys she likes in order to protect herself. As a result, she's typically pursued by men she isn't interested in, since she feels comfortable enough around them to be herself.

The coping style of moving away from others tends to occur in people who fear closeness and dislike depending on others. One study showed that people who tend to withdraw as a coping method were likely to expect their relationships to fail and were also likely to be less committed to their relationships (Birnie et al. 2009). Of course, less commitment to relationships typically results in fewer and shorter relationships. While sometimes it makes sense to take a bit of space or time away from a conflict, repeatedly withdrawing and not coming back to talk things through signifies an inflexible coping style.

Moving Toward Others

Maria is a people pleaser; she wants others to like her. She's considerate and caring, and she's always there for her friends when they need her. In her dating life, she tends to attract men who take advantage of her. She always feels that she's giving more to the relationship, trying to please the men she dates and make them happy with the hope that they'll come to appreciate her. But instead, Maria has become increasingly anxious about dating. The more she tries to please someone she's going out with—for example, going wherever he wants to go or changing her plans with friends to accept a last-minute date—the more anxious she feels about the relationship. She worries that if she lets her date down or makes any "mistakes," he'll lose interest in her.

Richard tends to move toward others once he's in a committed relationship. The more he feels invested in a partner, the more desperate he is for the two of them to spend all of their time together. He constantly wants to know how she feels about him because he worries that her feelings could change from one day to the next. Women tend to feel suffocated in the relationship, which only causes him more anxiety, and they always break up with him eventually.

If you tend to move toward others, you're more likely to develop anxiety and depression and are also more likely to have relationship problems (Jinyao et al. 2012). These problems often center around feeling insecure in the relationship, wanting constant confirmation that the other person is interested in you, and feeling overwhelmed by anything going wrong in the early stages of the relationship. When anxiety about a new relationship is so pervasive that it interferes with your ability to develop trust and intimacy, it means your coping style of moving toward others is inflexible. In addition, this craving for connection can have an opposite effect, as excessive reassurance seeking and attempts to please seem insatiable to others and end up alienating them.

Moving Against Others

Dallas has a strong personality and, in her words, prefers to "tell it like it is." She doesn't shy away from confrontation, and in dating situations, she tends to respond to feeling hurt or rejected by becoming aggressive or intimidating. Once, when a date called to cancel their plans because he was sick, Dallas told him, "Look, if you don't want to see me, just tell me the truth. I really don't appreciate being strung along."

Joey finds it off-putting when women expect him to pay for dates and be at their beck and call. His resentment tends to permeate all of his dates. Even with women who don't expect too much of him or are very kind, he tends to become defensive if he has even the slightest suspicion that he's being taken advantage of. Once, when on a first date with a woman, she innocently suggested to him that they grab a cab instead of walk to get dessert. He sharply replied, "I suppose you're used to being chauffeured around. Well, sorry to tell you, but if you're looking for someone to treat you like a princess, I'm not the guy. You can get your own cab, but I'm walking." Needless to say, there was no second date. In this way, Joey is moving against his dates, responding harshly if he thinks there's any chance he might be found lacking or be used.

Pushing others away is often done in an attempt to protect one's sense of self-worth. If you tend to move against others, you're probably more comfortable if you're in charge of every situation. You probably want to maintain control of your own emotions and control others' behaviors. You may approach relationships with a sense of competition and a strong need to be right. Being taken advantage of or exploited may be one of your top fears. Challenging others or intimidating them with anger helps you feel more competent and in control, warding off feelings of insecurity or helplessness. However, using this coping style can alienate others and sever relationships you may wish to maintain.

The Role of Avoidance in the Three Coping Styles

What all of these coping styles have in common is that they are used to avoid dealing with the anxiety that comes with dating. When people have trouble dealing with difficult internal experiences, like thoughts or emotions, it's common to try to avoid situations where these uncomfortable experiences occur (Hayes, Strosahl, and Wilson 1999). Avoidance is a key factor in anxiety, shyness, distress, and various psychological problems (Zinbarg et al. 1992).

Let's take a look at how avoidance played a role in some of the vignettes above. Brad avoided the anxiety associated with being close to and needing someone by withdrawing from women as the relationship became more serious. Likewise, Chloe avoided anxiety due to feeling vulnerable by acting coldly toward men she was attracted to. Maria didn't avoid romantic partners, but she did try to avoid feeling insecure or undesirable through excessive efforts to please her dates. By not putting herself in a position to get her own needs met, she also avoided anxiety around being rejected or feeling disapproval from her dates. For Joey, showing anger was a way to avoid the discomfort of feeling vulnerable to embarrassment, humiliation, or being taken advantage of. When avoidance of any type of discomfort takes precedence over connection, you'll have trouble developing the types of relationship you're looking for.

⎯⎯⎯➤ **Exercise:** Assessing the Costs of Avoidance

For some of the exercises in this book, I'll ask that you consider various questions and then write your responses. You may want to keep a special journal for these exercises. Use whatever you're most comfortable with: a notepad, loose-leaf paper, or a computer.

This exercise will help you explore the role of avoidance in your dating anxiety. Understanding the costs of your avoidance is a critical first step in finding love. Consider the following questions and sample answers, then write your own responses in your journal.

- What dating situations tend to cause you the most emotional or psychological discomfort?

  Example: I'm uncomfortable appearing too eager or interested in a guy. I don't want to seem desperate.

- List specific examples of times when you've used the coping styles outlined above: moving away from others, moving toward others, and moving against others. If you tend to mostly use one style, it's fine to list examples of just that one. For each example, think about what experience or feeling you were trying to avoid.

  Example: When I walked away from John at the birthday party, I was trying to avoid feeling uncomfortable and looking too eager. Seeming too eager would have felt embarrassing to me.

- How have efforts to avoid anxiety hurt your romantic life? List some examples. Perhaps you declined an invitation, reacted harshly to a date, or tried too hard to please someone.

  Example: Because of my efforts to avoid anxiety, I've missed out on getting to know John, as well as other guys in the past. Because of my fears, I have a lot of trouble showing my interest when I like someone.

Summary

In this chapter, you've increased your awareness of the role anxiety is playing in your dating life. It's helpful to remember that being shy, having social anxiety, or tending to withdraw from others isn't a life sentence condemning you to live in isolation. And now that you understand why your anxiety is so intense in certain situations, you can begin to move forward in ways that will help you be more comfortable getting close to others.

In chapter 2, we'll take a look at some of the most common dating worries, and I'll offer exercises that can be helpful for each. A key approach is to develop more awareness of the thoughts and emotions underlying your anxiety, and then to extend acceptance to those thoughts and feelings.

CHAPTER 2

——➤ ♥ ◄——

Help for the Most Common Dating Worries

On many levels, avoidance due to dating anxiety comes at a great cost. You may avoid some discomfort in the short term when you avoid situations that bring up painful feelings such as vulnerability or fear of embarrassment, but you ultimately end up feeling alone and trapped by your fear.

In this chapter, I'll discuss some of the most common dating worries and offer guidance on how to deal with them without using avoidance. This chapter is an introduction to topics we'll explore further throughout the book. It also gives you opportunities to start making changes right away. The overarching theme is learning a new way of relating to the uncomfortable feelings and inevitable suffering that dating brings up. I'll provide examples and exercises for each dating worry to help you understand both the theory and the practice of accepting your emotional state and feelings. Here are the worries we'll examine:

➻ Anxiety about rejection

➻ Fear of embarrassment

➻ Judging yourself or others harshly

➻ Anxiety about your appearance

→ Rumination on the past or worry about the future

→ Anxiety about sexual intimacy

→ Seeking reassurance or approval

The Compassionate View of Dating Worries

The worry, apprehension, and dread that come with dating anxiety and shyness are painful to experience. Part of knowing how to move forward and date more successfully is being able to acknowledge your fears without judging yourself or feeing ashamed. The worries outlined in this chapter are common, and experiencing these thoughts doesn't reflect any defect or flaw in you. Rather, these are simply ways you feel about dating; they are just part of your experience. Hopefully, understanding that others have similar worries will help you see that you aren't alone in your struggle and serve as a first step in extending compassion toward yourself for having these feelings of anxiety.

For each dating scenario, I'll offer suggestions about how you can view your anxiety from a more compassionate and accepting point of view. People are sometimes hesitant about extending compassion to themselves. But having self-compassion isn't about feeling sorry for yourself or making excuses. Instead, it's about looking at your own circumstances with kindness, caring, understanding, and concern. It means responding to your doubts, worries, and fears in a loving, gentle way, rather than with self-criticism.

Acceptance of difficult feelings is an alternative to avoiding them. Many people find the concept of acceptance a bit confusing initially. Having acceptance for your difficult feelings doesn't mean you want to revel in a particular experience or even stay in it. Rather, it means acknowledging the reality that you'll have a variety of experiences as you go through life—some joyful and fun, others sad, and yet others anxiety provoking and uncomfortable. You can't change your anxiety or make it go away on demand. You've probably already tried that, only to find it doesn't work. But you can acknowledge what's already there: an uncomfortable or upsetting thought or feeling. And with compassionate acceptance, you can change your reaction to your experience of anxiety by allowing anxious thoughts to exist without pushing them away or denying them. Increased acceptance has been shown to help decrease avoidance and improve quality of life (Eifert and Heffner 2003).

Accepting your inner emotional experiences is easier if you remind yourself that emotional states don't last forever. There's a natural ebb and flow to feelings. It's impossible to stay angry, humiliated, or fearful forever. As uncomfortable as some feelings may be, when you can accept that they are part of your current experience—which is always changing—you'll have less fear that you won't be able to tolerate the pain.

Anxiety About Rejection

Experiencing anxiety about being rejected by a potential love interest is one of the most common dating worries. If you're shy and anxious, you may have what psychologists call *rejection sensitivity*. This means that you're more likely to expect that potential romantic partners will reject you, and that you have a strong sense of anxiety associated with this expectation of rejection (Romero-Canyas and Downey 2013). With rejection sensitivity, you tend to interpret other people's cues as more negative than they are. You feel lonelier and disliked after any conflict, and expect that your relationships can't withstand emerging problems.

Elliot was highly sensitive to any perceived put-downs or slights from both friends and women he dated. It didn't take much for him to feel bad about himself. It was hard for him to take feedback from his boss without feeling criticized and like a failure. Most personal interactions felt unsafe to him because he was so sensitive to other people's comments and thought about even the most minor put-down for hours or days afterward. When dating, he often felt lonely, as if his dates didn't understand him or want to get to know him.

──→ Exercise: Evaluating Your Sensitivity to Rejection

To evaluate your level of rejection sensitivity, consider the following questions and write your responses in your journal:

- When talking with someone new, do you assume the other person is bored, uninterested, or only making conversation with you to be polite?

- Do you tend to notice and fixate on interactions where you feel put down or slighted? Do you tend to imagine slights from others? Do you tend to take these interactions very personally?

- When you enter a group of people, do you assume that you won't fit in or that the group members would rather you weren't there?

- Do you worry that people are being outwardly nice to you, but secretly do not like you?

- When you invite someone to connect on social media, like LinkedIn or Facebook, do you worry that the person will ignore your request?

- Do you think healthy and happy relationships come naturally to others but find it hard to imagine someone giving you the kind of love you see others receive?

- In conversations with others, does it seem they are criticizing you or finding fault with you?

- When others give you attention and seem interested in you, do you assume it's only a matter of time before they lose interest?

- When there's a conflict or problem in a relationship, do you assume it's the beginning of the end?

Now that you have a better idea of the kinds of situations that tend to trigger your rejection anxiety, you can start paying attention when these situations occur and tune in to your reactions. Rejection sensitivity can distort interactions, making them feel like a rejection has occurred (or will occur), even when that isn't the case. Bringing more awareness to these situations will help you note when your rejection sensitivity may be coloring your interpretations of other people's cues, causing you to distort the meaning of these events. In addition, identifying these situations can help you know when to implement the new coping skills you'll learn in this chapter.

Anticipating Rejection

Jessica typically expected to be rejected at any moment. She was interested in getting to know Todd, a coworker of her close friend Monica. But when Monica offered to set her up with Todd on a casual date for coffee, she immediately said no. She was sure Todd wouldn't be interested and would only agree as a favor to Monica. When Monica assured her that Todd seemed interested in going out with her, Jessica continued to hesitate. She worried that Todd would find her less attractive up close and feared that he'd feel let down. She got stuck in thoughts like *He doesn't know anything about me*, *He probably thinks I'm outgoing and funny like Monica*, and *He's sure to be disappointed in me*.

In the end, Jessica's fear of rejection was stronger than her desire to get to know Todd. The worried mind can be very convincing about how dangerous the future looks and how unkind others will be, and these assumptions are automatic. You probably find yourself bracing for the worst without considering more favorable outcomes.

Worse, these negative predictions actually impair your chances of finding love. When we expect something to happen, we tend to vividly picture how it will occur. Sometimes expecting rejection becomes a self-fulfilling prophecy. Studies have consistently shown that people who anticipate rejection end up eliciting rejection from romantic partners (Downey et al. 1998). You assume things will go wrong, and they do. For example, if you believe the woman you're dating is becoming less interested in you, you're more likely to behave in ways that will actually make her become less interested in you, such as withdrawing or being less affectionate toward her. Even if your initial feeling was incorrect (perhaps she just had a bad day and her feelings toward you hadn't changed), your expectation that she's losing interest can end up creating the very outcome you wanted to avoid. Because Jessica expected rejection from Todd, she didn't accept the date. The direct result was that Todd didn't pursue her.

Because every potential social interaction carries some risk of rejection, your social world can start to feel unsafe. You may become hypervigilant, always keeping an eye out for potential threats during conversations and being preoccupied with how likely it is that others are criticizing you or having negative thoughts about you. It's very painful to see the world from this viewpoint, as it causes you to feel that people are cruel and unloving. This may have been your experience in the past, whether in adult relationships or because of growing up with parents who were critical. And there are certainly many judgmental and critical people. However, most people you meet won't set out with the intention of tearing you down and finding fault in you. And if someone has expressed an interest in you, that person obviously wants to get to know you and see if the two of you might click. That person is hoping, just as you are, that things might work out.

Making Room for Other Possibilities

Even when someone seems to reject you, that doesn't mean the person is thinking the worst of you. If you ask a woman out and she says no, there could be any number of reasons. Maybe she's just ending a complicated relationship and isn't ready. Perhaps you're not her physical type. Maybe you remind her of an ex she'd rather forget. Maybe she's already seeing or interested in someone else. Or, it just might be that she's shy too and scared to say yes. The possibilities are endless, but it's important to consider them to help you see that an automatic thought like *She's rejecting me because she thinks I'm flawed* may not be accurate. There's a very real chance that you're causing yourself unnecessary suffering.

Yes, some people can be harsh when turning down a date. This is an unfortunate reality you may encounter. And in some instances, the person may indeed be having harsh or critical thoughts about you. But this is rare and doesn't reflect how the majority of people will view you.

Also, bear in mind that how someone treats you is a reflection of who that person is, not who you are. If someone is cruel toward you or makes harsh judgments about you based on a brief interaction, it reflects that person's inconsiderate behavior or judgmental predisposition, rather than being an indication of any shortcomings on your part. Therefore, if someone does respond critically or harshly toward you, you might consider whether that's really the kind of person you'd want to have a relationship with. Entering a relationship with someone who's hypercritical is a recipe for an unhealthy and unhappy dynamic, no matter how attractive or accomplished that person may be. In this case, you can view rejection as a blessing in disguise, saving you from going out with someone who's unkind.

➤ **Exercise:** Tuning In to Your Feelings with Acceptance

Even if you know that not everyone will reject you, the prospect of rejection may still seem terrifying. If you have anxiety, you're more likely to feel overwhelmed or threatened by your own negative emotions (Sauer-Zavala et al. 2012). This can cause even more difficulty with dating, since meeting a new person can activate so many strong feelings.

However, there is a solution. In this exercise, you'll learn to relate to your emotions differently, in a way that gives you awareness, insight, and choices about how to react to painful feelings. Rather than be held back by your emotions—running from them or letting them dictate your actions—you can create a space for them to exist, which will allow you to make thoughtful decisions about your behavior despite instinctive emotional reactions.

So often, the instinct in response to a painful feeling is to do something with that feeling: get rid of it, bury it, or avoid it. But with that approach, you can end up in an endless struggle to chase away feelings and never learn that you can handle whatever emotions life brings your way.

The best way to approach fear of rejection is to label what you're feeling, acknowledge those feelings, and then respond to them with a sense of openness, kindness, and compassion toward yourself. After trying the exercise outlined below, continue to practice it, using it whenever you start to notice anxiety-related fears and also in moments when you're not feeling particularly distressed. It's helpful to practice this exercise on a daily basis, even for ten minutes, so you can become accustomed to checking in with your own feelings and looking inward. (For downloadable audio version of this exercise, visit http://www .newharbinger.com/30031, or see the back of this book for more information.)

1. Begin by sitting in a chair in a comfortable position, with your hands at your sides, your legs uncrossed, and your feet firmly on the floor.

2. Close your eyes and move your attention toward your breath. Focus on the sensations of breathing: the cool air as you inhale, the warm air as you exhale, the expansion and contraction of your lungs, and so on. Continue to focus on your breath for a few moments.

3. Gently bring your attention to any feelings or emotions you might be experiencing. From an inviting, accepting perspective, open yourself up to whatever emotions may be present.

4. As you notice your emotions, gently label each feeling; for example, "There's the feeling of anxiety" or "I'm noticing the feeling of anticipation." There's no right way to feel and no state of being to try to achieve. Instead, allow your feelings to simply be. The purpose isn't to get rid of anxiety or feel differently than you do. Instead, this is a time to look within, discover the feelings that already exist within you, and just allow those feelings to be there.

5. As you notice feelings emerge, tune in to any tendency to judge those feelings—for example, *I hate feeling anxious.* When you notice judgments, try to label your feelings objectively: "I notice that I feel upset" or "I notice that I'm feeling distracted and irritable."

6. As you label your emotions, show that you're compassionate and open to whatever you may be feeling—for example, "I notice that I'm feeling anxiety. I accept this feeling of anxiety with kindness, caring, and compassion."

7. Before ending this practice, take a few moments to return your focus to your breathing. When you're ready, gently open your eyes and return to your day.

The first few times you practice this, you may notice yourself thinking, *Wait! I don't accept my anxiety or angry feelings with kindness! I want them to go away.* This is a natural response, but the truth is you can't always force emotions to go away. Sometimes they are just there, regardless of whether you want them or not. However, the process of labeling emotions in and of itself leads to lower levels of fear and anxiety (Kircanski, Lieberman, and Craske 2012), and will make your emotions less intense and intimidating.

As you begin to practice acceptance, you'll find that the urge to push away or deny these experiences lessens. Then, rather than fearing rejection, you'll learn that you can handle any momentary painful feelings that arise. And as you adopt a more accepting perspective, those emotions will begin to hurt less. In this way, exposing yourself to painful feelings and watching yourself tolerate them will give you confidence that you can handle the difficult feelings that come with dating.

Fear of Embarrassment

Pete had been trying online dating, and he'd been stood up twice in the past two months. The first time, he sat at the restaurant for forty-five minutes before calling it a night. He could see pity in the waiter's eyes as he asked, "Do you want to order something, or are you still waiting for your guest?" Pete never heard from the woman he was supposed to meet. The second time, Pete sat outdoors at an art walk on his own for thirty minutes before he texted his date to check in. He didn't get a response from her until the next day, when she e-mailed him and apologized, saying she'd gotten caught in a work meeting. However, she never rescheduled their date, and Pete had a feeling it was just an excuse.

Pete's feelings of intense embarrassment during the time he was waiting, and afterward as he recalled being stood up, were almost unbearable. He didn't talk to anyone about what happened, and his worry about being stood up and embarrassed again started to interfere with his ability to go on dates. He didn't know if he could handle feeling humiliated as he sat waiting for someone who might not show up.

When Pete came to therapy for help with his dating anxiety, we started by focusing on what we could do to reduce his investment in first dates. As he talked about the times he'd been stood up, it became clear that he'd gone out of his way to pick nice places to meet, even if it meant rescheduling work or driving a long distance. So the first step he took was to choose places that were convenient for him, close to either his work or his home. Then, if his date canceled or didn't show up, his routine wouldn't be greatly affected. This also reduced his anticipation and planning.

Next, Pete worked to increase the number of dates he went on in a given month. If he had several dates lined up, the prospect of one of them not working out seemed less catastrophic and more manageable. Scheduling more dates also meant he was less likely to build up any date with excessive anticipation or become overly invested in a woman before he got to know her.

Finally, and perhaps most importantly, we looked at Pete's response to his feelings of embarrassment. Pete discovered that his thoughts tended to be self-focused and overly critical. He was very concerned about his own appearance and what his date was thinking of him, and he felt that being stood up was a reflection of his deficiencies. His recurring thought was *If I were better, this wouldn't have happened to me.* As I worked with Pete to help him become a more objective observer of his experience, he was able to notice that being stood up wasn't a direct reflection of anything about him, and that it wasn't something he needed to beat himself up over. And once he gained some distance from his self-critical thoughts, he noticed that he felt less self-focused and self-conscious.

───→ **Exercise:** Learning from Feelings of Embarrassment

If fear of embarrassment is an issue for you (as it is for most people!), take some time to consider the following questions, then write your responses in your journal:

- When you feel embarrassed, what other emotions do you notice? What are you feeling besides anxiety and embarrassment?

- What types of thoughts do you have about yourself or others when you feel embarrassed? Do you consider some thoughts good or bad, or right or wrong?

- Look at the larger picture. What do you want from your dating experience? Does a particular embarrassing incident affect who you are as a person or the direction you're headed in life?

The purpose of this exercise is to help you become an objective observer of your own thoughts. This opens the door to responding to thoughts about feeling embarrassed differently. You may notice that, by looking objectively at the situation and viewing it through the lens of how the situation fits into your larger goals in life, embarrassing events typically don't have a significant meaning in terms of the kind of person you are and your worth or value. And they don't impair your ability to pursue your goals. One embarrassing incident, bad date, or no-show doesn't determine your future or your likelihood of finding love. In fact, most people would probably say that experiencing a few mishaps along the road to a good relationship is par for the course. Even the most confident people drop their forks at dinner or stumble over their words on occasion when nervous. It's helpful to reframe these embarrassing moments by viewing them as part of the path to finding the person you'll eventually be with.

Judging Yourself or Others Harshly

A judgment is a way of thinking that involves drawing a conclusion. In many ways, being able to make a thoughtful decision based on your judgment is an essential skill. For instance, it allows you to discriminate between a promising potential partner and someone with many red flags, such as a drug problem, commitment issues, and a history of infidelity. In this case, I think most people would agree that using your judgment is a good thing.

However, anxious daters have a tendency to be overly judgmental about others, and to assume their date is judging them harshly as well. This can get in the way of being open to new people, and it can also be misleading. For instance, consider the example of Renee. Whenever men gave her attention, she had the judgment that they were only interested in sex. And in some cases, she was correct; some men were interested in pursuing her solely for hooking up. However, several men she had dated were interested in more, but Renee's tendency to jump to conclusions prevented her from seeing this. Eventually, she started dating Conner, who was interested in a serious, long-term relationship. Even though Renee liked Conner a great deal, her initial generalized judgment that guys are only interested in sex prevented her from seeing him as anything but dangerous. Renee's judgment had become a wall surrounding her, keeping Conner at a distance. Fortunately, as time went on Renee was able to reevaluate her judgment and recognize that Conner was different from other men she had dated.

Zack, on the other hand, felt that women were always judging him based on his career as a capital investor at a financial management firm. He made good money, and he'd had several experiences where women appeared to be interested only in his wealth and the car he was driving. He began to judge women as shallow and superficial and felt burned out by the prospect of dating.

Both Zack and Renee had learned that, in the dating world, not everyone has the best intentions. Some people will be interested only in sex, and some will be interested in you for material possessions alone. But not everyone will have those narrow intentions. And eventually, both Zack and Renee had to learn that in order to find love, they couldn't let past experiences dictate their expectations of others.

Being guarded, especially when you're shy or socially anxious, is a natural state of being. A voice in your head says, *Proceed with caution. This won't end well!* Yet seeing the world as a dangerous place filled with ill-intentioned people can be harmful too, working against your best interests. Viewing the world through a harsh, judgmental lens tends to shut out everyone, including people who have good intentions.

An alternative is to recognize that you have the insight and awareness to evaluate each person and situation individually and recognize warning signs if they emerge. You can begin to look at dating as an opportunity to find someone you can trust and develop a mutually satisfying relationship with, while also being confident that you'll realize it if you're dating someone who is mistreating you or taking advantage of you.

——➤ **Exercise:** Practicing Loving-Kindness

This exercise is designed to help you move toward seeing the world and yourself with more compassion. It will help you open up to the feelings of loving-kindness that are so essential to giving and receiving love in a truly open way. Studies have shown that tuning in to feelings of loving-kindness can be one of the most healing, beneficial ways to improve your mood, relationships, and outlook on life (Emmons and McCullough 2003). When doing this loving-kindness practice, use whatever phrases work best for you. In the instructions below, I offer several alternatives. (For a downloadable audio version of this exercise, visit http://www.newharbinger.com/30031, or see the back of this book for more details.)

1. Begin by closing your eyes. Recall an instance when a friend, family member, or acquaintance said or did something that made you feel glad inside.

2. Capture that feeling of warmth and happiness. Allow it to live inside you, and feel it in your heart. Now extend that feeling out into your entire body. As you do so, say a phrase along the lines of "May I be healthy, may I find peace, and may I have joy."

3. Return to those feelings of gladness and send that loving energy out to a friend, using a phrase that conveys your loving intention—for example, "May you be happy, may you be healthy, and may you live with ease."

4. Send your loving-kindness energy to any member of your family and repeat the phrase—for example, "May you be loved, may you have peace, and may you have joy."

5. Spread the loving-kindness to your entire family—for example, "May all my loved ones be happy, peaceful, and free from suffering."

6. Find those feelings of loving-kindness again, and send them to your coworkers; for example, "May you be healthy, may you be happy, and may you have peace."

7. Extend your thoughts of loving-kindness to the entire state, then to the entire country, and ultimately to the entire world—for example, "May you find healing, may you have health, and may you have love."

8. Take a few moments to reflect on your feelings of gratitude and peace, and let these feelings resonate with you after the practice.

Judgmental thoughts tend to be negative and assume the worst in others or yourself. This loving-kindness practice will remind you that you have the capacity to be compassionate and kind. As you connect to these feelings within yourself, you'll find it easier to approach your everyday interactions in a way that embraces the good in others and in life.

When you're reminded about the love you have for people in your community, whether coworkers, friends, or family, it helps you see others as a source of joy and warmth. This is a good antidote to social anxiety, which tends to skew perceptions of the world, making others seem intimidating, scary, and harsh. By practicing loving-kindness on a daily basis, you become more attuned to others people's capacity for accepting and caring.

Anxiety About Your Appearance

For many of my clients who are anxious, their anxiety extends to worry about their appearance or certain aspects of their appearance. It might be a specific concern about skin, hair, body shape, height, or weight, or it might be about overall appearance. If you experience this, you may be painfully self-conscious about your appearance or fear that others will find fault with how you look or notice a physical flaw. When you meet new people, you probably wonder what they think about your appearance and worry that they may not like you because of your looks.

There's a term for the fear that you'll be negatively evaluated because of your appearance: *social appearance anxiety* (Hart et al. 2008). Some researchers suggest that one of the core fears in social anxiety disorder that causes people to fear public criticism is the belief that they have flaws in their appearance (Moscovitch 2009). Indeed, one study found that social appearance anxiety is a large risk factor for social anxiety (Levinson et al. 2013). If you have this type of anxiety about your appearance, it affects how willing you are to meet new people. It also affects the way you treat yourself and how you feel about yourself.

The first step in overcoming appearance anxiety is to recognize that this anxiety often causes distortions in how you see yourself. Just like a panic attack makes you believe you're dying or in danger, appearance anxiety makes you believe there are flaws in your appearance, although these perceived flaws probably aren't visible to others. Time after time, I've had attractive, nice-looking clients with appearance anxiety point out flaws in their appearance that I genuinely did not see or consider physically unattractive. So often, our evaluation of our appearance is more about the lens we see ourselves through, as opposed to the reality of what others see.

Also, keep in mind that the way you feel about your looks is often influenced by your mood and emotions. When you're feeling particularly critical or self-conscious about your looks, ask yourself how you're feeling inside. Many times you'll find that you're feeling discouraged, upset, overwhelmed, or lonely. These internal feelings can bleed into how you feel about your external appearance.

Your mood can even affect how you present yourself. In a recent study (University of Hertfordshire 2012), one hundred women were asked about what they wore when in different moods. About 57 percent of the women said they wore baggy tops when depressed, whereas only 2 percent did so when happy. They were also ten times more likely to wear a favorite dress when happy than when depressed (62 percent versus 6 percent).

Because of the link between mood and self-image, the second step in managing appearance anxiety is to tune in to your emotions. Ask yourself whether you're feeling bad about yourself and beating yourself up. Are you having trouble liking certain aspects of yourself outside of your appearance? Rather than continue to berate your appearance or worry about what others are thinking about how you look, stop and take a moment to gently reflect on how you're feeling. Do the exercise Tuning in to Your Feelings with Acceptance, from earlier in this chapter, and allow yourself to notice your internal state. Identify and label any difficult emotions you're experiencing. By acknowledging and accepting the emotions underlying your appearance anxiety, you can disengage from self-disparaging comments and instead cope with the underlying feelings. When you invite the underlying emotions in, it's usually easier to move on from being stuck in disliking the way you look.

My client Reagan tended to fixate on her appearance and things she hated about her looks. When she started doing the exercise of tuning in to her feelings, she noticed that her fixation on her appearance was often related to feeling bad about other aspects of her life: a fight with her mother, a work project that didn't go as planned, feeling nervous and insecure before a social event, or feeling lonely and disappointed that she had no plans for the evening. As she continued practicing tuning in to her emotions, she gradually became kinder to herself and learned to see her negative self-talk as a warning sign that something was upsetting her emotionally.

⟶ **Exercise:** Getting Unstuck from Appearance Anxiety

You'll probably find this exercise most helpful if you do it at a time when you're experiencing appearance anxiety. At that time, consider the following questions and write your responses in your journal:

- Are you overly focused on your appearance?

- What other emotions are you experiencing?

- In what ways is your negative self-talk related to your appearance hurting you?

Next, take some time to consider how you might decrease your negative self-talk, and then write about this in your journal. Recognize that berating yourself for your appearance isn't serving you well or helping you meet your goals. You may benefit from making a commitment to deal with the underlying feelings that are upsetting you. Another approach might be to choose to extend kindness and acceptance to yourself and focus on the positives about yourself and your choices in life.

Example: Rather than beating myself up, I can recognize I'm feeling badly because of my recent breakup. It will take time to heal from that relationship ending, and berating my appearance won't help me get over it.

Example: Putting down my appearance isn't helping me feel better. I'm committed to treating myself with kindness. I accept the things about my appearance that I can't change, and I embrace the things about my appearance that I love. I'm working to feel good about my appearance by exercising and dressing well, and I'm focusing on taking care of myself in other ways too. Above all, I'm working on liking myself, and that includes being comfortable in my own skin.

It takes practice to break the cycle of putting yourself down, but it's worth the effort. Your appearance is part of who you are, and learning to be kind to yourself and to truly like yourself—all of yourself—is important. There's nothing wrong with making an effort to enhance your appearance. A new haircut, wearing nice clothing, working out, and eating well—all can contribute to a sense of taking care of yourself and liking who you are. But the essential approach is learning to focus on being kind to yourself, handling the emotions underlying your appearance anxiety, and ending self-condemnation.

Rumination on the Past or Worry About the Future

Have you ever noticed that anxiety tends to be about what could potentially happen or what might go wrong in an imagined future scenario? Generally, anxiety tends to manifest in the form of worry about the future, rather than concern about what's currently happening. For instance, you might worry about what to write in a text to someone you like because you're not sure how your words will affect that person's response to you. In this case, you worry about what could happen if you say the wrong thing and whether your actions will have negative consequences: *If I say the wrong thing, it's all over.* These kinds of what-ifs can become paralyzing as you spend a lot of time wrapped up in future-oriented thoughts rather than living in the present.

Conversely, anxiety can also manifest in the form of *rumination*: the process of focusing on things from the past that cause distress, and thinking about them over and over again. This is common among people with shyness and social anxiety. You focus on past encounters that feel like failures, replaying how a conversation went, what you said, and how the other person responded. You may spend time thinking about what caused you to develop such sensitivity to anxiety and wonder why you can't be more like other people who just let things go. And because rumination keeps you stuck in the past, focused on regrets or trying to figure out what went wrong, it also makes it difficult to live in the moment.

The well-known Serenity Creed is useful with both future- and past-oriented worries. It says, "Grant me the serenity to accept the things I cannot change, the courage to change the things I can, and wisdom to know the difference." Rumination and future-oriented worry are often focused on things you cannot change or control. You can't necessarily control the level of anxiety you'll have when meeting new people or going on dates. You'll probably always experience some degree of anxiety. However, it's extremely powerful to recognize what you can do to take control: you can choose to meet and open up to new people, and you can choose the kind of person you want to be.

Likewise, you can't control what others are thinking or how they'll respond to what you say, but you can control how you behave and the words you choose to use. You can't control the worries or nerves you'll feel from time to time, but you can control what you do or say when you experience those worries. In other words, you can choose to let anxiety keep you stuck, or you can choose to move on despite the anxiety. Similarly, you can't control whether a date likes you, but you can control your own values and what you like in others. And while you can't always choose how people treat you, you can choose the kind of person you want to be and how you wish to treat others. Ultimately, you can't change the past or control the future, but you can live each day with appreciation and dignity.

——→ Exercise: Identifying What You Can and Cannot Change

The following exercise will get you unstuck from worry by helping you decide whether you can change something or not. You can complete this exercise in your journal, or visit http://www.newharbinger.com /30031 for a downloadable version. (See the back of this book for instructions on how to access it.)

1. List as many of your worries, fears, and concerns as you can think of.

2. Label each worry or concern "current problem," "future problem," or "past problem."

3. Divide a fresh piece of paper into two columns. Title one column "Things I can change or influence" and the other "Things I cannot change or influence."

4. Put each worry, fear, or concern into one category or the other.

This exercise is useful in several ways. Simply compiling a list of your worries helps you be aware of where you're spending your energy. Labeling whether worries are about past, current, or future problems offers some insight into how often you are or are not in the present moment. It also indicates how much time you spend worrying about things that are inherently beyond your control because they've already happened or may not even transpire. Breaking the list into two columns will help you decide where to focus on acceptance (things you cannot change) and where to take action (things you can change). When you find yourself worrying about something that you cannot change, gently remind yourself that worrying probably won't help resolve that problem, then allow yourself to move on from thinking about it.

Anxiety About Sexual Intimacy

Many shy people struggle with physical intimacy (Rowsell and Coplan 2013). You may very much want to be physically close to the person you're dating but feel unsure about how to initiate sexual advances. You may be uncertain of when the timing is right. How long do you wait to kiss her? How can you tell if he's interested? How do you know if you're coming on too strong?

There are no definitive answers to these questions. These things often depend on the people involved and the circumstances. For that reason, these kinds of questions can create a great deal of uncertainty, which heightens anxiety. After all, uncertainty is typically anxiety's nemesis: anxiety wants to know the right answer, and it wants it now. However, dating doesn't often offer certainty, especially during the early phases.

Mindfulness can be helpful in these situations, allowing you to focus on the here and now and let go of some of the distress associated with uncertainty. By tuning in to the moment, you'll deepen your awareness of your own feelings and desires, and be more sensitive to your partner's signals. Rather than getting stuck in questions, you'll be able connect with your date and your own experience, and make decisions on a case-by-case basis. You can make subtle advances, notice your partner's response, and be okay with the outcome of those advances.

You may also feel some anxiety about your ability to enjoy sexual encounters in the early stages with someone new. This anxiety, which affects both women and men, typically comes from external sources, such as media and social messages about how you're supposed to perform or the ideal way to look, but it can also come from within (Dove and Wiederman 2000). In addition, shyness can reduce arousal or the ability to enjoy sexual encounters (Karafa and Cozzarelli 1997).

Another issue regarding sexual intimacy that can cause worry is deciding when the time is right. Part of the evolution of a relationship is bringing your relationship into the physical realm and deciding whether you'll be exclusive. When people hook up without commitment, the resulting feelings can vary. One study found that 78 percent of women and 72 percent of men who had noncommitted sex experienced regret about it (Fisher et al. 2012). However, other studies have shown that people have positive feelings after a hookup, with one study finding that 82 percent of men and 57 percent of women were generally glad they had hooked up (Garcia and Reiber 2008). Yet another study showed that having a one-night stand or hooking up without any commitment led to increased feelings of embarrassment, loss of respect, shame, regret, and emotional difficulties (Lewis et al. 2012).

Being in the moment and fully present with someone sexually is a wonderful part of a relationship, and this is typically easier when you're close to someone in the context of a good relationship (Garcia et al. 2013). When sex is rushed or is the only connection you have with someone, it can sever your connection to your sexuality, making it feel less meaningful and pleasurable. You might be rushing into things because you think that's what's expected, want to keep your date interested, or believe that it will help you connect with the other person. I've seen many people proceed with a sexual relationship before they were comfortable with it, and this often leads to problems. For example, it can bring out intense emotions early in a relationship, and those feelings may not be reciprocated.

On the other hand, developing true sexual intimacy with your partner is a gift. Sexuality is a natural and wonderful part of being in a relationship, and one you should enjoy when you feel ready. Emotional intimacy and sexual intimacy tend to be intertwined and foster each other. Becoming more comfortable in your sexual identity can help you open up and share affection with your partner in a way that can be essential to a fulfilling relationship.

──→ **Exercise:** Exploring Your Sexuality

For many reasons, you may not have taken much time to consider your sexual identity. Perhaps it brings up overwhelming worry. Or you may have received the message early in life that "nice guys" or "good girls" don't have sex or want sex. This exercise will help you begin to understand your sexual history and explore your feelings about sex and sexuality. Take some time to consider each question, then write your responses in your journal:

- How did you first learn about sex? How did you feel about what you learned?

- When did you first notice feelings of sexual attraction?

- What kind of sex education did you receive? What did you learn from your parents, siblings, friends, or teachers about sexuality? How did you feel about learning this new information?

- What was your first sexual experience with another person like? What was your motivation for having sex? Was it an intentional decision or spontaneous? How did you feel afterward?

- If you haven't experienced sexual intimacy with another person, what are your thoughts and feelings about having sex with a partner in the future? What emotions does this idea bring up?

- Have you had any trauma surrounding sex, such as rape, incest, abuse, or negative experiences? How have you dealt with those painful experiences?

- What cultural messages have you heard regarding sex and gender? How do you feel about those cultural messages?

- In what situations do you feel most confident sexually? What is it about those situations that you enjoy?

- Have you had a one-night stand, a hookup partner, or friends with benefits? What are your feelings surrounding these encounters?

- Have there been times when you've felt inhibited about showing physical affection? What were the circumstances?

- Have there been times when your thoughts or worries distracted you and prevented you from enjoying physical intimacy with a partner? What sorts of thoughts or worries did you have?

- How does your body image play into how you feel about yourself in sexual situations?

Considering and answering these questions will help you start to think about your sexuality as simply another aspect of who you are. You can begin building a healthy sexual identity by allowing yourself to explore and integrate your sexual and sensual needs and desires, and by getting comfortable with those needs and desires. For many people, the optimal goal is to approach sex in a way that makes them feel valued and respected while also being free to enjoy their sexuality. Because sexuality is such a foundational aspect of intimate relationships, chapter

7 offers more in-depth strategies for becoming comfortable in your sexuality, dealing with anxious thoughts during intimacy, and developing a good physical relationship with your partner.

Seeking Reassurance or Approval

In romantic relationships, Hannah almost always felt anxious and on edge. She noticed a pattern: as she started getting closer to a new man, her anxiety would flare up. It was difficult for her to tolerate the uncertainty inherent in a new relationship, and sometimes she sought reassurance and approval from partners before either of them really knew where the relationship was headed. Men seemed scared off by her need for approval and reassurance so early in the relationship.

This is a fairly common pattern. If you have lower self-esteem, you're more likely to seek excessive reassurance from friends and romantic partners, which can end up turning them off. When seeking reassurance, you may say things like "I feel like we aren't getting together this week as much as we did last week. Are you upset with me?" or "Is everything okay between us?" If you ask these kinds of questions excessively, a new partner may feel overwhelmed or intimidated.

Having a strong need for approval or reassurance may stem from doubts about your level of worthiness. You may worry that your partner doesn't reciprocate your feelings. You may wish for a sense of merging, believing you'd feel less anxious if there were no distance between the two of you. And while this kind of merger might make you feel more connected, it can cause you to lose your sense of self and sabotage your relationship. You may begin to feel dependent on your partner for your identity, and your partner may back away. Ultimately, this will alienate your partner and drive you apart, rather than making you closer.

➤ **Exercise:** Finding Alternatives to Neediness

Feelings of self-doubt, uncertainty, or anxiety are easily triggered in a new relationship and can lead to excessively seeking approval and reassurance. This exercise will help you identify specific behaviors and words that you might use in an effort to obtain reassurance, and that may cause you to feel overly dependent on a new romantic partner's approval. Once you've identified these patterns, you can replace them with new, more effective behaviors.

1. To begin, identify specific situations in which you're most likely to seek a new romantic partner's input, advice, or approval. For example, do you change plans at the last minute to accommodate the other person's schedule? Have you made drastic changes in your life for a new love interest?

2. Next, try to pinpoint the underlying emotion you're feeling when you're tempted to ask for reassurance or approval. For example, is it fear, worry, self-doubt, or emptiness?

3. Finally, identify three or four alternative behaviors you could use when you're tempted to seek approval or reassurance or make drastic changes to accommodate a new romantic partner.

    Example: I could make the decision without asking for his input, and instead rely on my own opinions and desires.

    Example: When I notice that I want reassurance or approval, I'm going to take ten minutes to slow down and pay attention to where I am emotionally and physically. By practicing mindfulness, I can notice the urge to seek approval and become aware of how anxiety is affecting my decisions.

Summary

This chapter addressed some of the most common dating worries and began to suggest some solutions. The following ideas summarize the most common ways that anxiety can leave you feeling stuck in dating. These points also lay the groundwork for the solutions we'll explore in the upcoming chapters.

Getting stuck in your head: Buying into unhelpful thoughts about dating, your ability to date, and not being good enough can get you stuck in your own mind. The acceptance practice in this chapter and mindfulness practices you'll learn in later chapters will help you form a new relationship with your thoughts. Rather than getting caught up in critical and self-defeating ways of engaging with your own thoughts, you'll be able to extend more kindness, acceptance, and tolerance to your thoughts about yourself.

Getting stuck in your emotions: Your style of reacting to strong negative emotions, such as feelings of insecurity, shame, fear, embarrassment, resentment, or anger, can affect your success in dating. You may feel overwhelmed by these emotions or try to avoid them because of how uncomfortable they make you feel. Instead, I encourage you to accept the emotions that are already there. Label them and allow them to be, which will help them diminish in intensity more quickly. Then you can move on more easily.

Getting stuck in not knowing what you want: Because anxiety can be so powerful, your whole life may revolve around managing your anxiety. This doesn't leave you with much time or energy to work on things you might care about in life. Consider this: what would you do differently in your life right now if anxiety weren't a factor? We'll explore this question in depth in chapter 5, as this is essential for getting what you really want from life, love, and a partnership.

Getting stuck in inaction or hurtful action: Anxiety and shyness can be paralyzing and painful. But withdrawing from the world and avoiding anyone who could possibly hurt you will keep you stuck in the same rut: shy, single, and wishing for love. Anxiety can also lead to hurtful actions; you may share too much or demand too much because of your nerves, or you may hurt yourself by giving too much. Whether the problem is inaction or hurtful action, the antidote is learning to slow down, evaluate your options, and make choices based on your values rather than knee-jerk reactions. The mindfulness skills you'll learn in later chapters will help you move in this direction.

Getting stuck in a role: We all have stories about who and how we are: *I'm not the kind of guy girls like. I'm always too needy in relationships. I'm just a shy person.* Yet these kinds of statements tend to be limiting, telling us what we can and can't do and what we expect life to give us. This can make you feel incapable of having the kinds of relationships you truly want. In the next chapter, you'll learn skills that will help you gain some perspective on these kinds of thoughts, rather than being fused with them. In the process, you'll develop a more flexible sense of identity that will allow you to be an active participant in choosing how you want to live.

CHAPTER 3

➤ ♥ ◄

Are Your Thoughts About Dating Holding You Back?

Madison and Ethan ran into each other when dropping their kids off for day camp. They chatted about their plans for the upcoming weekend: Madison said she was taking her kids to the zoo, and Ethan said he was starting to train for a half marathon.

Madison, a thirty-nine-year-old single mother of two, hadn't been on a date since her divorce was finalized a year and a half ago. Her husband, John, had begun a new relationship several months after he separated from her and recently married the woman he had begun dating. Madison felt betrayed that he had moved on so quickly and easily.

Ethan was a single dad and had never been married. He thought Madison was a wonderful mom and found her intriguing. Every time he saw her, he tried to find a way to talk with her.

As Madison stood and chatted with Ethan, she thought to herself how pleasant he was to talk to and how she'd like to be around him more. *Nonsense!* She automatically reprimanded herself. *Ethan is just being friendly. He doesn't want to date a divorced single mom.*

Then Ethan said, "Well, I hope you have fun at the zoo. You should check out the marathon info and think about signing up. We all train together, and it's a great experience."

Madison felt uncomfortable and her hearted started racing. She wasn't sure what was happening. Was Ethan just being polite, or did he want to find a way to spend time with her? She didn't want to read too much into his comment for fear of embarrassing herself. She thought it best to brush it off, rather than seeming eager or possibly misinterpreting his intent. So she said, "Oh, okay. Sure," and abruptly turned to leave.

Even though Madison was drawn to Ethan, she tended to get caught up in anxious thoughts about dating, and these thoughts had popped up during their conversation:

- *No one wants to deal with my baggage. I'm emotionally damaged and hurt from my divorce.*

- *There are no good men out there. Even the ones who seem kind will only hurt me.*

- *I don't know if I'll ever find love again. I had my one shot at love with my husband, and it didn't work out. Maybe love just isn't in the cards for me.*

Because Madison bought into her thoughts and acted accordingly, she was unable to respond to Ethan in a way that might have led to a friendship or romantic relationship. Instead she withdrew. And although Ethan was confident and persistent, he eventually got the message and stopped trying to get to know her.

❣

The thoughts you have about yourself, dating, and others can play a huge role in preventing love from entering into your life. This chapter will help you start relating to your thoughts in a new way. Rather than viewing them as absolute truths, you'll learn to gain some distance from them and a new perspective on them.

Understanding Anxious Thoughts

Our thoughts are a continual stream of words that help give meaning to the world around us and help us make sense of our experience. They're a running commentary that we each have inside our heads.

One effect of anxiety and shyness is that your thoughts become hypercritical, hyperaware, and sometimes intrusive. Anxiety can also make your thoughts more extreme, or black-and-white. Sometimes anxious thoughts are rational, but often they aren't. The difficulty is, anxious thoughts *feel* full of meaning and induce a sense of dread; the threat feels very real. So having the anxious thought *I can't go on this date* may bring up such powerful feelings that you truly believe you can't go on the date.

One of the keys to getting past anxiety is being able to see that the thoughts in your mind don't always accurately reflect what's happening in the outside world. They are just one interpretation of events, sort of like a commentator reporting on a political debate. Of course, the commentary differs depending on the political affiliation of the commentator. In much the same way, your thoughts are probably at least a bit biased based on the experiences you've had in the past. This bias becomes problematic when anxious thoughts are so pervasive and strong that they take control of how you respond to situations.

Defusing from Anxious Thoughts

Cognitive defusion is the process of bringing awareness to thoughts and detaching from them so that they don't rule your behavior and, in the case of negative thoughts, don't produce or intensify negative feelings. Defusion allows you to see your mind as a machine that produces thoughts; from this perspective, you don't have to attach excessive significance to those thoughts or view them as literally true.

An important part of defusion is recognizing that you can't always change what your anxious thoughts say. They're likely to pop up regardless of whether you try to stop them: *I shouldn't have said that, I won't fit in, She's way out of my league, Coming here was a huge mistake, I can't handle group settings, I really hate dating,* and on and on. But what you can control is how you respond to these anxious thoughts. Do you believe them? Do they upset you? Do you act on them? In other words, do your anxious thoughts lead to an anxious behavior?

When you're feeling highly anxious, it's easy to relate to your thoughts as if they were actual, real-life events, rather than recognizing them for what they are: just thoughts. For example, say you see someone you like on an online dating site and decide to send a message. Immediately after you hit "send," you have the thought *Oh no! That was a really stupid message and she's going to hate it. I blew it.* This is just a thought; it may or may not be true, and it probably isn't the exact response the person will have to reading your message. But if you're fused with your thought, you'll have the same emotions and feelings as if the person had in fact read the e-mail and replied, "This is a really stupid message. You blew it." Similarly, if you're having a panic attack and you're fused with the thought *I'm having a heart attack,* you'll experience the same level of fear you'd have if you truly were dying from a heart attack.

When you're able to recognize that your thoughts are separate from the events they refer to, you can more easily accept your thoughts for what they are: passing thoughts—no more, no less. This is cognitive defusion, and the exercises in this chapter will help you learn to do just that.

Handling Anxiety About Anxiety Symptoms

Thoughts about physical symptoms of anxiety, and particularly whether they're visible to others, can be preoccupying and distracting: *Am I blushing? Is my voice shaking? Oh, my palms are starting to sweat. My anxiety is really starting to show.* In addition, you may heighten these symptoms by constantly monitoring what's happening around you, scanning for warning signs of potential embarrassment: *Is everyone in the group getting along but me? Do I fit in? Is he trying to avoid talking to me now because of how awkward I'm acting?*

Paying close attention to physical symptoms of anxiety—blushing, sweating, shaky voice, rapid heartbeat, and so on—is understandable. You may hope that by doing so you can prevent your anxiety from growing. Unfortunately, what happens is just the opposite: constant monitoring makes small signs of anxiety seem bigger or more frequent and makes you even more anxious. It's like a snowball rolling down a hill, with one anxious thought leading to another and overall anxiety gaining momentum and getting larger.

➤ **Exercise:** Becoming a Distant Observer

A helpful approach to hyperawareness of anxiety symptoms is to observe yourself as you monitor your own thinking process (Hayes 2005). Instead of responding to your thoughts with more anxious thoughts, take the stance of being a distant observer. As a distant observer, you can be aware of when you start to notice your anxiety symptoms without buying into your anxious thoughts. This exercise will help you develop that perspective. Try it the next time you notice physical symptoms of anxiety and nervousness about them. Here I'll use blushing as an example.

When you feel yourself blush, you might normally have a thought like *My cheeks are bright red. This is awful. Everyone knows I'm embarrassed.* Instead, observe your reaction as if from a distance, saying to yourself, "I'm having the thought that it's awful to blush and have people know I'm embarrassed." Rather than placing a judgment on your experience (*It's bad to blush; people shouldn't know I'm embarrassed*), simply note the experience without judging it. Blushing becomes just blushing—neither good nor bad, neither desired nor undesired.

Whenever you notice anxious thoughts emerging, use the format "I'm having the thought that _____." For example, "I'm having the thought that he's judging me" or "I'm having the thought that I shouldn't be feeling this way." This phrasing creates some distance between yourself and your thoughts so they become less anxiety provoking. It helps you remember the difference between buying into a thought and just having a thought (Luoma and Hayes 2003).

You may also notice that when you allow yourself to have a thought without buying into it, you begin to experience your interactions with others differently. You're freer to just be in the moment and experience the situation. You'll feel more comfortable about doing and saying what you really want to do and say because you have less fear of anxious and self-critical thoughts looming over you. Whereas blushing may have previously sent you into withdrawal mode, with defusion you can give less weight to the thoughts provoked by blushing and move on with your conversation.

This technique is helpful with any type of thought. I recommend practicing it often with difficult thoughts until it becomes second nature.

⟶ **Exercise:** Watching the Anxiety Snowball

This is another exercise that will help you gain distance from your thoughts. It's a meditation technique I developed that helps you visualize the act of observing your thoughts as they pass through your mind.

1. When you notice anxious thoughts feeding one another, gently distance yourself from the worry by saying to yourself, "There goes the anxiety snowball."

2. Observe what the snowball of your thoughts is doing; for example, "I can see my anxious thoughts building up and gaining momentum" or "Now I see the thought *My heart is beating out of my chest* being added to the snowball."

3. Continue to watch the snowball. Each time you have a thought, sum it up in a simple word, like "anxiety," "judgment," or "boring." Place each thought onto the snowball.

4. Notice which thoughts cause the snowball to grow. Don't try to block or resist the snowball by pushing the thoughts away. Simply allow your thoughts to come, and then gently place them on the snowball, watching as it becomes separate from you and rolls farther and farther away.

5. Imagine that the snowball comes to a stop. The anxious thoughts may still be there, but you notice the snow starting to melt, your anxieties dissipating and becoming less dense. As the snow melts, your anxiety-related thoughts hold less and less weight.

This practice serves as another reminder that your thoughts are not you. You don't have to get caught up in the snowball of anxiety. Instead, you can just observe the snowball as it goes through the natural process of gaining momentum and growing, then slowing, stopping, and melting. Just like a snowball, your anxious thinking doesn't last forever, and it will eventually run its course. You'll notice that your anxious thoughts lose much of their power and momentum when you observe them from a more dispassionate perspective.

Handling Thoughts That Lead to Dating Burnout

Dating burnout can happen after one bad date or after a series of unsuccessful dates or relationships. The common theme in dating burnout is an overwhelming feeling of wanting to give up, accompanied by thoughts like *Dating isn't worth it* or *Love will never happen for me*. If you've ever felt this way, you are not alone! And just the simple knowledge that you aren't the only one who feels this way can help you feel less isolated and sad.

It's also helpful to know how anxiety and shyness can add to dating burnout. The purpose of anxiety is to help you avoid danger, hurt, or pain; its job is to protect you. Therefore, your anxious thoughts will try to convince you of all of the ways dating isn't safe or isn't worth it—and that it's better to give up than to face another bad date. The depression that comes with shyness and anxiety can add to the sinking feeling that love will never work out for you.

Dating (or the lack of dating) can definitely be discouraging at times. I don't expect you to deny how hard it can be. For instance, not hearing from someone you like can be painful. Allow yourself to acknowledge the feelings of being discouraged and hurt. At the same time, unfailingly accepting thoughts like *It will never happen for me* is a way in which thoughts get fused to your sense of self. Learning to detach yourself from these thoughts can help you recognize both that it's okay to feel upset and that you don't have to believe this holds any significance in terms of your actual dating prospects.

⟶ Exercise: Thanking Your Mind

One way to get distance from some of your more discouraging thoughts is through the simple but powerful exercise of thanking your mind (Hayes 2005). Since your mind is trying to protect you from feeling worried, hurt, or disappointed, you can acknowledge its efforts and thank it for providing you with discouraging thoughts. When you notice a thought like *Love will never happen for me*, you can reply, "Thank you, mind, for trying to protect me by telling me that love will never happen for me." This is an effective way to remind yourself that you can have discouraging thoughts without buying into them.

Understanding the Roots of Self-Critical Thoughts

Starting a new relationship often means being vulnerable. But when you don't feel good about yourself, it feels overwhelming and intimidating to open up. At the core of anxiety, there's often a deep sense of shame—a feeling that you're flawed or defective at your core. These feelings of shame often develop at an early age.

Sometimes shame begins with being bullied or ostracized at school, which can leave a lasting feeling of being alone, defective, or an outsider. Similarly, parents or other family members may evoke feelings of shame in kids throughout childhood. For instance, your parents may have tried to teach you a lesson by saying something like "Look what you've done to your sister. You made her cry!" As a child, you probably didn't fully understand how your actions affected others. If you heard that you'd done something wrong without understanding why or how, this probably made you feel like you were inherently bad. Adults often talk about feeling unworthy because of childhood experiences in which they felt they somehow failed to meet the expectations of a stern, strict, or emotionally unavailable parent. A pervasive sense of shame can arise due to being neglected, abused, or shamed as a child (Zimbardo 1982). In addition, a deep sense of shame can develop in adulthood, brought on by being emotionally hurt by past partners.

To some degree, everyone has experiences that can trigger shame. However, some people tend to respond to shame by turning their pain inward and becoming more focused on painful inner experiences. It's also common to feel self-critical about feeling shame. In this way, shame can become part of your self-view, causing you to see yourself as flawed and generating numerous self-critical thoughts.

The first step in healing this sense of a flawed self is to acknowledge that, yes, people have hurt you, and that you didn't deserve this. Mean kids at school, family members, or former partners may have said or done things that made you feel inferior, but that doesn't mean you're inferior, weak, defective, or broken. The second step is to break the cycle of self-critical thoughts in response to feelings of shame. To do so, it's crucial to respond to harsh, critical thoughts about yourself with a nonjudgmental compassion (Gilbert and Procter 2006).

⟶ **Exercise:** Reframing Your Perspective on Your Past

This exercise will help you form a new relationship with painful past experiences and allow you to move on. In this approach, you extend self-compassion and acceptance to self-critical thoughts and feelings. *Self-compassion* means approaching yourself with caring, nurturing, and loving-kindness, and as discussed, acceptance means being able to recognize that there are certain things you can't change, including the past. Rather than responding to shame with further feelings of self-loathing, you acknowledge the shameful feelings you experience and accept them without berating yourself for feeling the way you do. You're effectively ending the fruitless struggle to deny your experience and acknowledging your thoughts without overidentifying with them. Then, instead of fueling a cycle of shame, you can respond to shame with much-needed self-compassion.

Take some time to consider the following questions, then write your responses in your journal. I've provided example responses from Christina, a forty-one-year-old mother of two who's been divorced for one year.

- Consider your personal history. What painful experiences have you had in relationships? List the areas of your life that bring up self-critical thoughts and describe those thoughts.

  Christina: My marriage and divorce from my husband bring up self-critical thoughts. I think I'm a failure because my marriage didn't work. I think there's something wrong with me because I couldn't keep us together.

- Identify the emotions you feel in response to these self-critical thoughts.

  Christina: I spend a lot of time feeling ashamed and regretting the years I spent with my ex (but not the fact that we have two wonderful kids). Mostly, I feel sadness and a sense of loss.

- Identify and describe a new, more compassionate perspective toward your emotions. It may be helpful to imagine a person who embodies wise, compassionate, and nurturing traits and how this person might respond.

  Christina: It's understandable that I'd feel sadness and a sense of loss after my divorce. I'm working toward finding compassion for my emotions of sadness. My divorce doesn't define me as unworthy or unlovable. I am a lovable, worthy person.

- Identify and describe a new, more accepting perspective toward your past experiences. Again, it may be helpful to imagine a person who embodies warmth, understanding, and acceptance, and how this person might view your circumstances.

> *Christina: I can't change the past, but I can accept it and find a sense of peace and calm about my divorce. I can accept this as part of my history and acknowledge the pain that it has brought without turning that pain into self-critical thoughts about myself.*

For Christina, finding a new way of viewing her divorce was a healing experience. It allowed her to let go of her regret and see herself in a new light: her divorce was part of her past, but it didn't define her. With time, she was able to let go of self-critical thoughts about her divorce, and this helped her feel ready and able to look for a new relationship.

Completing this and other exercises in this book is an act that signifies your willingness to move in a new direction in life. Being willing to disengage from self-critical ways of thinking is one of the most important steps you can take. And as with acceptance, willingness isn't about being perfect and never feeling anxious. Rather, it's about taking a different stance toward your experiences, both internal and external, not getting stuck in self-critical thoughts, and extending loving-kindness to yourself. What regrets are you ready to let go of?

Dealing with Overly Self-Conscious Thoughts in Dating

The way you talk, the way you dress, how you look, the kinds of questions you ask, the way you answer questions, the way you laugh, how you order a meal, what you choose to do on a date—when you're shy and anxious, all of these are areas in which you may be particularly self-conscious and critical.

Self-conscious thoughts often come out in a postmortem, when you're reviewing a date or going over an interaction with someone after it happened. As you replay what happened, you may be highly critical of yourself. This is highly demoralizing, painful, and upsetting. People often have a tendency to criticize themselves through the eyes of others (Leary, Kowalski, and Campbell 1988). This is a form of *mind reading*, in which you assume you know what others are thinking and, in this case, that their thoughts about you are highly critical. You may assume that someone you like is thinking the worst of you, which heightens your self-consciousness and self-criticism. It also leads to self-blame, in which you assume a conversation or interaction didn't go well because of something you did or said. Indeed, research has shown that shy and anxious people tend to take more responsibility for negative social outcomes than those who aren't anxious (Hoffman and Teglasi 1982).

——➤ **Exercise:** Labeling Self-Conscious Thoughts

In order to turn overly self-conscious, critical thinking around, it's helpful to label the types of thoughts you're having about yourself, using labels like "judgment," "evaluation," "anxious thought," "self-critical thought," and so on.

To illustrate how to do this, I'll use Trevor as an example. He went to a party where he ran into Bianca, whom he'd been interested in for a few months. He'd been hoping to see Bianca and get a chance to talk to her again. But when he saw her at the party, he got nervous and waited until the end of the evening to approach her. They chatted and it seemed to go well. As she left, Bianca said, "Good to see you. Next time come talk to me earlier!"

When Trevor got home that night, he couldn't stop berating himself: *What did she mean by that? I'm such a wimp, I should have talked to her sooner. Why did I wait so long? Was I staring at her all night? It must have been totally obvious I wanted to talk to her. I bet I seemed creepy to her.* But Trevor had recently started working on learning to label his thoughts, and when he realized what he was doing, he tried that tactic, telling himself, "I'm having the critical thought that I'm a wimp" and "I'm mind reading when I assume Bianca thinks I'm creepy."

Labeling self-conscious thought processes in this way helps reduce their negative impact. Whenever you notice that you're being self-critical, use this technique to label your thoughts, then respond with compassion, as described in the next exercise.

———➤ **Exercise:** Reflecting on Your Dating Experiences with Compassionate Attention

I recommend doing this exercise after every date or significant social encounter you have. For the purposes of doing it now, recall a recent social interaction or date that elicited harsh, self-conscious, or critical thoughts about yourself, then take some time to consider the following questions and write your responses in your journal. I've provided examples from Todd, who was feeling highly self-conscious after a date with Simone.

- Write out an objective outline of your experience: What happened? Also identify your favorite parts of the experience and the most unpleasant or anxiety-provoking moments.

  Todd: I went out with Simone last night. I decided to take her to a French bakery since her mom is from France. She told me she loved the place, so it felt great that I had chosen well. I was really nervous at first, but after the first ten minutes I started to feel okay. We walked around town after eating our desserts and had a good time talking. I made her laugh—that was my favorite part of the date. At the end, I tried to walk her to her car, but we got lost. I couldn't find the street the bakery was on, and it was super embarrassing.

We found it eventually using her phone, but by that time I was flustered and felt like an idiot. Because I was thrown off, I wasn't able to keep talking normally, and I think she noticed. I had been thinking about giving her a good-night kiss, but things got so awkward and I was stuck in my head, so I didn't try.

- List any critical thoughts you have related to yourself or your behaviors during that experience.

Todd: I was kicking myself the whole way home. I shouldn't have gotten lost; it made me look stupid. And then I didn't kiss Simone because the moment didn't seem right, and I ruined the whole thing by being too much in my head. The perfect time to kiss her would have been as we were walking around town, laughing and talking. She was sort of looking up at me and slowing down, and that would have been the perfect time, but I froze up.

- Write an alternative response to your critical thoughts, using a perspective of understanding and kindheartedness, and gentler language.

Todd: A kinder, more caring way to look at it is that no date goes exactly perfectly. Getting a little lost isn't going to make or break a date. I mean, if Simone liked me before, she probably wouldn't stop liking me just because of getting lost. And as for no kiss good-night, there will be another chance to show her how I feel. Being physically affectionate is something that takes me a little time, but it's also okay to act on how I'm feeling in the moment.

- Write a compassionate response to any fears you may have about how the experience will affect the future, or describe what you learned from the experience. Try to phrase it in a positive, caring, and empathetic way.

Todd: I'm worried Simone will think I don't like her, but I can show interest by calling her tomorrow to ask her out again. And next time, I guess I might remind myself that it's okay if things don't go perfectly—we can still have fun. I also want to work on being confident and showing her physical affection in those moments when it seems like we're both on the same page.

By retelling your story objectively and noting your favorite and least favorite parts, you can get a more well-rounded sense of how the date went. Critical, self-conscious thoughts tend to mask everything else. The good moments fade away, and it almost feels as though they didn't happen. With this exercise, you see the full picture and your attention is drawn to the areas in which you interacted successfully.

This exercise also reminds you to view your experience with compassion and to use less harsh, critical language when recalling your experiences, which is beneficial in many ways. Higher self-compassion is linked to increased connectedness with others (Neff 2003), higher levels of life satisfaction (Neff, Kirkpatrick, and Rude 2007), and lower levels of depression (Leary et al. 2007). Extending compassion to yourself is also a proven, effective way to reduce the negative effects of self-critical thoughts (Neff 2003). As you practice journaling from a caring, compassionate perspective after each date and significant social encounter, you'll begin to integrate this kindness into the way you think about yourself. In this way, you'll start emphasizing the best in yourself and in others, seeing the human condition of struggle, error, and shortcomings with kindness while also opening your heart to moments of happiness and contentment.

Lifting the Burden of Expectations

In dating, there's undeniably a certain amount of pressure, and this can definitely fuel anxious thoughts. There's pressure (often self-imposed) to be witty, to keep the conversation going, to ask questions, to make fun plans, to look good, or to show your best self. All of those expectations can bog you down, create anxiety, and prevent you from truly being yourself on dates. I'll let you in on a secret: your date wants to impress you too. It's helpful to remind yourself that conversation is a two-way street. Half of the responsibility is the other person's. Imagine taking all of the pressure you feel and giving half of it to your date. Rather than focusing on high expectations of yourself, pay attention to your date. Get to know him, observing how he responds to your interests and questions, and see whether he's someone you'd like to get closer to and have fun with.

Thoughts About How and Where You Should Meet Potential Partners

Anxiety and shyness will try to dictate what you're comfortable with in terms of dating. I find that people who are shy or socially anxious are the most reserved in terms of how, when, and where they're willing to meet new people. I challenge you to let go of such rules and instead try to embrace new situations that may help you find someone you really care about.

My client Addison, an attractive, bright, twenty-nine-year-old woman, had been single for over a year and a half after a long-term relationship. She was convinced that there were no good guys left and that it was virtually impossible to meet someone. She told me, "Most of my friends are either already in a relationship or married, or they're having just as much trouble meeting someone as I am. I'd rather not do online dating. There are too many weirdos there, and just looking at profiles makes me anxious and dizzy. And I don't want to do any of those 'just lunch' or 'speed dating' things. The only people who go to those are pathetic and lonely. I don't want to join a club or activity just to meet someone; that seems awkward. And I can't imagine asking my friends to set me up, because it's embarrassing to ask for that."

Addison had a lot to offer a potential partner, but her thoughts about dating were getting in her way and preventing her from meeting new men. She was so fused with her thoughts and certain they were correct that she closed herself off to many avenues for meeting men.

In our work together, I helped Addison begin to see her thoughts as simply one way of thinking about things, rather than an absolute authority. With time, this allowed her to try some speed dating and lunch dates, despite her thought *Only pathetic and lonely people do that, and it won't work anyway.* Eventually, she set a goal of meeting a wide variety of men and regularly putting herself in situations where she might meet someone new (always safely, of course). When her anxious mind said something like *The party will be too stressful and a waste of time* or *There aren't going to be any interesting men there*, she acknowledged those thoughts and then went anyway. And as she increasingly understood that she didn't need to act on her anxious thoughts and rules about dating, she developed a mantra: "A thought is just a thought—it doesn't make it true." By suspending her judgments, Addison gave herself the opportunity to try new experiences that she formerly would have avoided.

When Addison employed her new mantra and became more comfortable socializing with potential dates, some interesting things happened. As she became more self-confident, she noticed that there *were* decent men who were interested in her—online, through social apps, and at social events. Receiving attention initially brought up some anxiety for her, but she also found that the more she interacted with men who were interested in her, the less it made her anxious. In addition, she finally felt like she was doing something that gave her a good chance of meeting someone compatible. This brightened her spirits and made her more approachable. And when men did approach her, she found it easier to talk to them and be friendly.

In time, Addison met someone she really liked: Landon. He was polite, considerate, funny, and attractive. They dated for over seven months. In the end, they found that they weren't compatible for a long-term relationship, but by then, Addison had come to realize that there are indeed good guys out there. Landon wasn't pathetic, weird, or creepy; he was just a nice guy who wanted to meet a woman to potentially have a relationship with. So even though the relationship didn't work out, Addison felt that she was on the right track and making progress toward finding someone who would be a good fit.

The Judging Mind

Right now you may be thinking, *This Addison woman's story is nice and I'm very happy for her, but her experience is nothing like mine and doesn't sound realistic to me. I've been to parties and tried online dating, and the experience hasn't been good.* You wouldn't be alone in having reservations about whether other people's experiences have much bearing on yours. But I'd like you to notice that this is a judging type of thought. In other words, this is just one way of perceiving and relating to Addison's story. You can notice your judging thoughts for what they are by saying, "Now I'm having a judgment about how likely it is that any of this dating stuff can work for me."

By noticing that this is a judgment and creating distance from the thought, you can begin to see for yourself that thoughts don't have to predict your actions. Instead, you can bring attention to your judgments and then decide that, despite your doubts, you don't know for sure that some of the strategies Addison used won't work for you. You could decide that your thoughts don't have to dictate what you do and set up an action plan along these lines:

1. Let your friends know that you're open to being set up on a date if they have someone in mind.

2. Accept all invitations and attend all social gatherings you're invited to.

3. Sign up for an online dating service.

4. Actually go to the site and respond to messages you receive.

5. Accept a few dates for coffee, even if you're not sure how they'll go.

6. Attend the dates you agree to.

7. Work to notice and defuse from judging thoughts throughout the process.

Depending on whether you want to dive right in or take small steps, you might start with steps 1 and 2, or you might just commit to steps 3 and 4. Either way, the eventual goal is to engage with the world around you as much as possible with the intention of not letting anxious thoughts get in the way.

Part of what happens when you start to get some distance from your thoughts is that they have less power over you. Another part is that you begin to tolerate different outcomes. You start to care a bit less about what happens if someone doesn't call, since you no longer believe it means you're undesirable. You assign less importance to the actions of others because you recognize that your thoughts about what happened, such as *He doesn't like me, I blew it, I'm not pretty enough,* or *He's too good for me,* aren't necessarily accurate. You also begin to recognize that you may never know why a date didn't work out, but that it's okay to not have all the answers. And even if you like someone and it doesn't work out, you become more accepting. This flexibility allows you to consider the idea that one person doesn't define you, your dating potential, or your lovability.

Lastly, and significantly, you begin to embrace your new, more flexible ways of thinking and act on them by making changes to your dating behaviors. In the rest of this chapter, I'll outline ways that you can increase the number of people you meet by increasing how comfortable you are initiating contact, responding to dating requests, and facing fears of any social mishaps that may occur.

Initiating Contact

My client Cameron, a forty-five-year-old divorced father, found the concept of dating again terrifying. He had married his high school sweetheart at nineteen, and she had been his first and only long-term relationship. He told me, "I'm not good at initiating contact with women. I don't know how to show interest without coming on too strong. And I hate the idea of being rejected."

Many shy people have similar struggles, feeling uncomfortable talking to new people, let alone being the one who initiates contact. Yet this is one of the best places to start following your desires rather than being ruled by anxious thoughts. You can initiate contact in many ways: striking up a conversation, giving a compliment, sending someone an e-mail through social media, meeting someone at a sports event, introducing yourself to someone at a party, talking to the person next to you in line at the bank, and so on. The key is to take that first subtle yet significant action that shows someone you're interested.

The nice thing about initiating contact with new people is that the risk is relatively low in terms of rejection. After all, if the person doesn't respond positively, you don't have a lot invested in the relationship, so it shouldn't be as painful. In fact, with meeting a new person, a more realistic expectation is that it very well may not work out. I recommend that you take as many opportunities to practice initiating contact as possible. The more you do so, the more skilled you'll become and the less pressure you'll feel. Plus, if you don't meet new people, it will be awfully hard to establish a relationship or fall in love.

As I worked with Cameron, who worried about coming on too strong, we focused on how he could initiate contact in a way that was friendly and a little flirtatious but also played to his strengths. Cameron was a naturally funny guy, so he worked on using humor and lightheartedness when making contact with new women.

He also set a goal of initiating contact with one to three new women each day, just to practice meeting women. He usually started in the morning at a coffee stand, where he would smile or say a quick hello to a woman while standing in line or waiting for his coffee. If she smiled back or said hello, he might respond with a casual, friendly comment. Next, he used his lunch break as an opportunity to initiate contact. He tried to make conversation with women in the elevator. If he went out for lunch, he'd chat with a waitress or hostess. In the evening, he might initiate contact with someone at the gym, such as a woman next to him on the treadmill, or he might say hello to a woman standing next to him in line at the grocery store.

When doubts and anxious thoughts crept in during these overtures, Cameron took the stance of an objective observer and labeled his thoughts, then reminded himself that he was in control, not his anxiety. He adopted the mantra "I refuse to let anxiety stop me from doing what's meaningful in my life."

What was most important as he practiced making contact was that he remained true to who he was. Rather than trying to pretend to be someone else to meet the expectations he imagined women had, he focused on speaking to them in a way that genuinely reflected his personality. In time, he gained confidence and felt more comfortable expressing his personality and even his inner thoughts. He discovered the parts of himself that he liked best and shared them with women he was interested in. He told me, "Women may or may not like me, but either way, I'd rather have a woman like me based on who I really am."

And in time, Cameron wasn't as nervous about coming on too strong. From all of his practice in initiating contact, he'd learned how to make subtle overtures that he was comfortable with. He'd also gotten good at telling whether a woman was eager to chat—a signal to move forward—or wasn't receptive. He noticed that some women were aloof and uninterested, but that others were quite receptive, smiling and seeming flattered when he talked to them. He found it refreshing to know that there were women who were kind and pleasant—and a few who definitely seemed interested in getting to know him. And most powerful of all, Cameron's fear of rejection had diminished significantly and no longer affected his ability to reach out to people.

⟶ **Exercise:** Practicing Making Contact

You can work on getting more comfortable making contact with others by setting a goal similar to Cameron's, initiating interactions with others on a regular basis. These need not be people you're interested in romantically, and you can choose people of any gender for this practice. Here are some daily or weekly goals you might choose:

- Smile and make eye contact with three people each day.

- Smile and say hi to everyone you pass during a half-hour walk.

- Say hello and make a conversational remark to someone waiting next to you in line.

- Approach someone who's walking a dog and ask if you can pet the dog.

- Have one conversation with a stranger each day: a mechanic, waiter, clerk, barista, or florist—anyone you come into contact with during your day.

Once you've completed your goals for a week or two, begin to focus these interactions on people you're attracted to or potentially interested in. Applying the same principles, continue to approach the interactions in a lighthearted, casual way.

Being Receptive to Contact

Many women—and some men—prefer not to initiate contact and would rather wait for someone who's interested to approach them. If this is true for you, you'll want to work on being receptive to outreach from others and finding ways to increase opportunities for others to initiate contact. This requires that you notice when others are sending you signals that they're interested, and that you be open to their outreach—if you are indeed interested. So when someone strikes up a conversation with you, contacts you online, or generally shows interest in you, don't let your shyness or anxiety make you appear uninterested or aloof. Many of my shy clients say they aren't very comfortable receiving attention, especially initially. Unfortunately, this can keep them from showing when they like someone.

Increasing Receptive Behaviors

However, you can start to show interest while also staying true to who you are, shyness and all. My client Lily, a young woman in the field of computer engineering, provides a good example. Because her shyness and anxiety caused her to feel uncomfortable with new people, she responded by saying very little. Many of her friends had told her that she seemed distant and aloof when they first met her. Likewise, men have thought she was snobby or cold, when in reality she's a very tender, warmhearted person. But even when she wanted to talk to a potential love interest, she wasn't sure how to proceed.

For a while, she had been particularly interested in Elijah, a man who lived a few doors down in her apartment building, and she was fairly certain that he liked her. They often talked by the mailboxes, and Elijah offered to help her with small chores and such, but Lily didn't let their conversations go on too long.

Lily discussed her interactions with Elijah in session. She realized that she tended to cut off their conversations, leading to fewer interactions with him even though she wanted to talk more. Lily said she liked Elijah but wasn't sure how to convey that to him. We discussed strategies she could implement during their conversations to show her interest in small ways. She started by not ending their conversations so quickly. She also began asking Elijah more questions about himself and accepted his offer to help her carry in her groceries. She showed interest by allowing herself to enjoy his company, and in time, she started feeling more comfortable around him. One day when he flirted with her, she allowed herself to be flattered and she smiled, which also showed her interest. At the end of that conversation, Elijah asked Lily to go out with him the next weekend, and she accepted.

In session, we discussed how she felt about accepting the date offer. Even though the prospect of going out with Elijah made her nervous, she resisted her initial urge to say no because she knew she liked him. She chose to accept some of the uncomfortable thoughts and feelings associated with the date in order to gain the opportunity to spend more time with Elijah.

Another way to think about showing interest is to ask yourself, "If I had a magic wand that made all of my anxiety disappear, how would I respond to this situation? What would I want do or say if anxiety weren't an issue?" (Hayes 2005). The goal is to have your outside behaviors match your values—what you really care about in life. It's a good way to gauge when it's time to accept your anxiety in order to follow your desire to get to know someone.

Being Receptive Without Being Overeager

As you begin to respond to others' overtures, you may wonder how you can show interest without feeling too vulnerable or eager. This was definitely an issue for Melinda, a twenty-five-year-old nursing student, who came to see me after a fairly new boyfriend, Nolan, had broken up with her. She had always been shy, so she usually waited for men to ask her out or make the first move. But once they did, she often found herself becoming very interested, very fast. Her anxiety made it hard for her to take it slow.

She'd met Nolan through an online dating site, and once they started seeing each other, she always made sure she was available when he wanted to get together. She wanted to see him, and she worried that if too much time passed went between dates, he'd lose interest. Soon she started sending him text messages or Facebook messages the day after their dates, often asking when she'd see him again. But Nolan wasn't asking her out as frequently, and she felt like he was losing interest in her. This made her even more anxious and eager to please him, and she ended up feeling on edge when they were together, trying to do and say the "right" things to make him like her. She bought gifts for him and drove out of her way to go see him. Before long, Nolan stopped calling her altogether and didn't return her messages. Then, a few weeks later, he told her he wasn't ready for a committed relationship.

That's when Melinda came to see me. This wasn't the first time this sort of thing had happened, and Melinda was worried that her eagerness was driving men away. As we began working together, it quickly became clear that her anxiety was behind many of her overeager behaviors. Her need to know when she'd see Nolan again arose from her uncertainty about how he felt about her. I helped her see that in the early stages of dating it's natural to have some uncertainty. It takes time to get to know one another and see how things might progress.

As Melinda learned to tolerate some of the anxiety and uncertainty that came from waiting to hear from men, she realized that she actually felt less insecure when her dating experiences were a two-way street. She gained confidence as she realized how good it felt to maintain her dignity in this way. And while she still showed the men she dated that she was interested in them, she was able to dial back her intensity level. Her new approach also allowed her to better gauge how interested her dates were in her, since she gave them time to reach out to her first.

Coping with Fears of Social Mishaps

Shy and socially anxious people often have elevated concerns about potential social mishaps: inconveniencing others, being seen as weird, being thought of as unintelligent, or being the center of attention and embarrassing themselves. Do any of the following worries sound familiar? *What if I talk to her and she thinks I'm totally weird? What if I respond to his comment and he thinks I'm not smart? What if I talk to her and she finds it annoying and bothersome?* These thoughts tend to be accompanied by predictions of catastrophe: *I'll embarrass myself and it will be a disaster.*

A technique called *social mishaps exposure* can help. It involves intentionally creating and facing feared situations in order to learn that social mishaps don't lead to long-term, irreversible, or negative consequences. One study of social mishaps exposure (Fang et al. 2013) provides a good example how this works. One participant in this study was Mary, who had several fears relating to social situations. She was given an assignment for each fear. For example, for her fear of losing her place while giving a speech, she purposefully paused for more than five seconds in the middle of a speech. For her fear of being the center of attention and inconveniencing others, she interrupted a group of people at a restaurant and asked to practice a maid-of-honor speech. To target fears of being the center of attention and being seen as weird, Mary went out on the street while wearing bandages on her face and asked people if they were Carl Smith because his car was being towed. These kinds of experiments helped Mary see that no real harm came from doing these things, and by the end of treatment, her anxiety symptoms had decreased by almost 60 percent.

⟶ **Exercise:** Practicing Social Mishaps Exposure

When practicing exposure to fears, it's important to choose situations that provoke at least moderate anxiety and to stay in the situation until your anxiety begins to subside, allowing you to learn that the consequences aren't as disastrous as you fear. You may find it useful to do some exposures repeatedly, noticing how your level of anxiety tends to decline with each practice. You can conduct exposure to social mishaps in a variety of ways. Here are some suggestions, but feel free to develop and engage in your own exposure situations:

- Open an umbrella inside a public building and walk around.

- Do a cartwheel outside a movie theater. Then walk backward slowly toward the ticket line.

- Get in a crowded elevator and face the back of the elevator.

- Approach a group of people at a restaurant and ask if anyone has the time. When they answer, pause for five seconds, then say, "I'm late!" and rush off.

- Head to a library or bookstore. Put a book on your head as you browse, holding it there for several minutes.

- Go to a restaurant at lunchtime and sit down at a table for two. Tell the waiter you're waiting for a friend. After twenty minutes, go ahead and order and eat your meal alone.

- Go to a department store and engage a salesperson in a long discussion about various clothing items. Try on the clothes, ask about them at length, and then leave without buying anything.

- Go into a coffee shop wearing brightly colored, mismatched clothing. Order coffee and sit and read a newspaper or magazine for fifteen minutes.

- At a bookstore, approach someone browsing the aisles. Ask for some book recommendations for a birthday present for your niece.

- Stand next to a post office and ask people where you can find a place to send a letter.

- Attend a movie dressed up as the main character.

- In a crowded park, walk backward for thirty seconds with your arms extended straight out at your sides. Slowly do a complete 360-degree circle, then do a jumping jack and continue on your way.

The goal is to see for yourself that nothing awful happens with these behaviors. In fact, you might have fun or strike up an interesting conversation. In all likelihood, the worst that will happen is someone giving you an odd look. Typically, people either don't pay much attention to the behavior, or are very friendly and helpful regardless.

This technique works because, rather than avoiding embarrassing situations and the catastrophic consequences you imagine might happen, you face those situations and the fears associated with them head-on. Most importantly, it helps you gain more freedom and flexibility in interacting with others. You also become less sensitive to other people's reactions. Instead of monitoring others for even the slightest hint of disdain or disapproval, you learn to accept what others think of you and feel less need for their approval. This is truly freeing.

In dating, this will help you build confidence and become more open. Fear is replaced with confidence, caution is replaced with ease, and rigidity is replaced with flexibility. This sense of self-assuredness will enhance your ability to initiate contact or be receptive to outreach from others.

Summary

This chapter discussed some of the ways thinking can get in the way of your dating experience and helped you discover how developing a new relationship to these thoughts can open you up to new, more flexible ways of interacting. It also offered strategies for acting on your desires despite your anxious thoughts by initiating contact, being open to contact from others, and overcoming fears of social mishaps.

The next chapter will give you more strategies to increase your dating skills and flexibility by helping you develop your capacity for mindfulness. Being present in the moment will help you connect with yourself and also help you connect with your dates.

CHAPTER 4

Engaging with Your Date

Parker, a shy young man in his late twenties, had a way of making Megan feel listened to and understood. She could tell he was paying attention to her and really cared about what she had to say. On their two dates, Parker had learned a lot about Megan. He'd also shared his thoughts and opinions about a wide range of topics. This was a breakthrough for him. In the past, he'd had difficulty connecting with women due to his intense worry that he'd say the wrong thing or offend them, and when he was around women he found very attractive or desirable, his anxiety paralyzed him. But after Parker started practicing mindfulness, he began to approach his worry in an entirely new way. As a result, he was more able to engage with his dates, and with Megan, he established a strong connection quickly.

❣

When you're shy or socially anxious, it can be hard to truly connect with your date. You may be distracted, have a tendency to second guess what you said, or walk on eggshells to avoid "messing up" and ruining the date. This chapter can help with all of those problems. Practicing the mindfulness skills you'll learn here will help you be more aware of the present moment, decrease your focus on worry, and increase your openness to whatever the moment brings. In this way, curiosity (and often acceptance) begins to replace worry and fear. All of this will help you forge a better connection with your own emotions and with your dates.

Mindful Awareness

To give you an idea of what mindfulness is, let's first take a look at what mindfulness is not. When you're driving your car on the freeway and miss your exit because you're lost in thought about something your boss said to you at work, this is the opposite of mindfulness. You're far away from your here-and-now experience, in both place and time. Likewise, you can get caught up in thoughts about the future, like thinking about what you'll have for dinner while exercising at the gym. Being caught up in a TV show or a movie is similar: you forget about your current reality and get lost in a different world.

In contrast, *mindfulness* is the process of being keenly aware of and attuned to the present—to your here-and-now experience. Mindfulness is purposefully choosing—moment to moment and day to day—to pay attention to your experience and be in the world as it is. And by extension, *mindful acceptance* is the process of responding to your here-and-now experience, including thoughts, feelings, and urges, nonjudgmentally and with openness and kindness.

They key to mindfulness is bringing a nonjudgmental sense of curiosity of the moment. Mindfulness isn't about how things should or shouldn't be or wishing things were different than they are. It's about accepting what's already there and letting it be.

Being in the present moment is a skill that helps you engage with others as you bring that same nonjudgmental attention and curiosity to your interactions. You can connect because your thoughts aren't off in another time or place, which serves as a barrier to intimacy. Research has shown that practicing mindfulness meditation regularly results in lower anxiety, a more positive self-image, and an increased ability to cope with stress (Hoge et al. 2013). Moreover, mindfulness has been shown to contribute to making relationships stronger, closer, more secure, more satisfying, and more understanding (Atkinson 2013).

──▶ Exercise: Practicing Mindful Breathing

A good way to get a feel for mindful attention is to be in the present moment with your breath. This classic mindfulness exercise may seem simple, but it can be both challenging and enlightening. (For a downloadable audio version of this exercise, visit http://www.newharbinger .com/30031.)

To begin, find a comfortable, quiet spot where you can either sit comfortably or lie down without being disturbed. Lie or sit with your hands at your sides and your legs uncrossed.

Close your eyes and take a few moments to notice how your body feels as you bring your attention inward. Notice any sensations in your body and the sensation of your breath. Notice the natural flow of your breathing, in and out. There's no need to try to make your breaths longer or deeper; instead, simply pay attention to what your breath is naturally doing. Gently notice how your body shifts as you breathe in and out: the rising and falling of your belly, and the feeling of air passing through your mouth or nose.

Bring a sense of acceptance and openness to your experience. There's no right way to feel or ideal state to achieve. Just notice your breath and its effect on your body. Your mind will probably start to wander away from noticing your breath, thinking about plans for the day or getting lost in a daydream. When you notice your attention wandering, gently bring your focus back to your breathing. The act of noticing your attention wandering is, in and of itself, an act of mindfulness. You're in the moment, recognizing that your thoughts have left the present moment. This is an opportunity to extend patience and kindness toward yourself. Remind yourself that it's natural for thoughts to wander, then gently bring your mind back to the present moment.

Continue to practice mindful breathing for at least five minutes. As you end this practice, slowly widen your attention and gently open your eyes. You'll probably feel a renewed sense of connection to your body. Enjoy this and bring it with you through the rest of your day.

Mindful breathing is a great practice for becoming more connected with your thoughts, sensations, and inner being. Even just five minutes a day is a good start. In time, you may want to practice more, especially if anxiety is an issue for you. Research has shown that practicing mindful breathing for forty-five minutes daily for eight weeks can significantly reduce anxiety (Hofmann et al. 2010).

This type of exercise is a form of meditation, the repetitive process of focusing your attention, noticing that your attention has been pulled in another direction, and then bringing your attention back to the original focus. Research has shown that practicing meditation regularly promotes brain growth in key areas related to relationship satisfaction (Atkinson 2013). Mindfulness can also contribute to successful relationships by enhancing open awareness, empathy for others, and the ability to regulate your mood and physical reactions to emotions.

Mindfulness of Emotions

Dating is rife with mixed emotions and uncertainty: *Does she like me? Will he call? Should I tell her how I feel about her?* For those with anxiety, mixed emotions can be difficult, especially during the early phases of dating, as demonstrated by Lily's story in chapter 3. This is because the anxious brain interprets uncertainty as a sign that something is wrong. At its core, anxiety is about feeling threatened and in danger when you don't know what the future holds.

Because anxiety feels overwhelming and often takes center stage, it makes it hard to pay attention to other feelings, including your other feelings about dating. But consider this: If you could focus on emotions other than anxiety when dating, what might you find? Would you perhaps notice a degree of excitement? Might you find a sense of hopefulness about the potential of a particular relationship? Though anxiety may be persistent and loud, don't let it fool you into thinking it's the only emotion you have about dating.

The truth is, it's natural to have a wide range of emotions about dating, and about life in general. But one of the common traits among people with anxiety is a strong sense that they shouldn't feel how they feel: *I don't want to feel so nervous. I wish I didn't feel so frustrated. Why do I feel so much pressure? Why can't I just feel normal?* While this urge to banish negative or unwanted feelings is natural, it can hurt your ability to get past these emotions. The more you resist feeling this way, the more upset you'll feel. Studies have shown that denying or trying to avoid upsetting emotions leads to greater anxiety, whereas being accepting and tolerant of those emotions leads to less distress (Kashdan, Zvolensky, and McLeish 2008).

As a culture, we tend to teach men to not show their feelings, equating emotions or displays of emotion with being weak or effeminate. For women, there's the fear of being labeled overly emotional, crazy, or difficult. Many people think that if they can just ignore or suppress emotions—*voilà!*—they'll disappear. But realistically, that's not how it works. Anxiety, fear, or worry will still be there, despite efforts to get rid of it.

Consider Michael. He tried to ignore overwhelming emotions, but this caused him to act in ways he later regretted. If he felt rejected by a woman he liked, he tried to get his mind off it by going out drinking with friends. After a few rounds, he usually ended up calling or texting the woman several times in a row without waiting to hear back from her. Sometimes he left messages that were unpleasant or angry. The next day, he felt embarrassed about those calls because they didn't reflect who he was or how he really felt.

The alternative to ignoring, resisting, or trying to numb your emotions is to approach them with mindful acceptance. Once you embrace your emotions rather than pushing against them, their power over you will begin to diminish. Then you can decide which coping skills you want to use to deal with difficult emotions, and choose what action you want to take, if any, regarding the cause of your emotional turmoil.

——→ Exercise: Practicing Mindfulness and Acceptance of Emotions

This exercise, which incorporates concepts related to urge surfing (Marlatt and Kristeller 1999) and dialectical behavior therapy (Linehan 1993), will help you practice mindfulness of emotions and open the door to accepting them while not acting on any urges they bring up. (For a downloadable audio version of this exercise, visit http://www .newharbinger.com/30031. See the back of this book for more details.)

Start by recalling a recent time when you experienced a painful emotional reaction related to a particular person or interaction. Even if the interaction is relatively fresh in your mind, try to place yourself back in that moment, recalling the details and the emotion you felt. Holding that experience in mind, take the following steps:

1. **Label the emotion.** Begin by gently closing your eyes and bringing your attention to your body. Label the emotion you're experiencing, saying its name to yourself; for example, "Embarrassment....There is embarrassment." Try to note where, if anywhere, in your body you feel the emotion: "Anxiety....There is anxiety. I feel it in my chest."

2. **Rate the intensity.** Next, rate the intensity of the emotion on a scale of 1 to 10, with 1 being least intense and 10 being most intense.

3. **Look for willingness to feel the emotion.** See if you can call up willingness to feel the emotion rather than pushing it away, ignoring it, or criticizing yourself for feeling this way. Are you able to give yourself permission to feel the way you feel? Rather

than wishing it weren't so, can you allow yourself to stay with the emotion?

4. **Practice acceptance of the feeling.** Acknowledge that while you may prefer not to have this feeling, you can't deny what's already there. Allow yourself to look at the emotion and your experience of it with kindness and compassion, recognizing that all emotions are a part of the human experience. Affirm your acceptance to yourself. For example, say, "Frustration.... I recognize my frustration and extend compassion and acceptance to myself. It's a natural emotion and I don't need to hide from it or deny it."

5. **Note any urges related to the emotion.** Is the emotion accompanied by a desire or urge to do something about it? Do you feel compelled to fix, stop, or dismiss the emotion? Label any urges. For example, "Now I notice that I have the desire to _____." Fill in the blank with whatever urge you're having: "to get out of here," "to distance myself," "to call him again," and so on.

6. **Ride out the urge.** Note that just because you have an urge to do something with the feeling doesn't mean you must act on that urge. Instead, you can simply notice the urge and ride it out. Affirm this to yourself. For example, "I have the urge to call him, but that doesn't mean I have to act on it" or "I have the urge to cancel my blind date tonight because I'm feeling discouraged, but I don't have to cancel the date just because I feel that way."

I recommend using this technique often; you can do so anytime you encounter a difficult emotion. As you practice simply sitting with difficult emotions, you'll probably notice that feelings are like waves crashing on the sand: they ebb and flow. Although you may be feeling negative emotions in the moment, they'll probably fade soon, making way for other emotions. Understanding this can help you be willing to feel an emotion without acting on any urges that may accompany it.

Opening the Door to Positive Emotions

Extending mindfulness and acceptance to difficult emotions also has the benefit of helping you better connect with other, more positive emotions. When you accept difficult emotions rather than struggling against them, they no longer hold as much power over you; their effect is diminished. This leaves room for emotions like joy, happiness, mischievousness, appreciation, confidence, daring, and playfulness to emerge. In addition, you'll notice and identify these positive emotions more easily because you're more in touch with your inner experience.

Paying attention to your feelings will also help you connect with yourself and be emotionally aware. In addition, you'll be in a much better position to have positive experiences with the people you go out with. This emotionally balanced perspective can vastly improve the outcome of your dates, especially when combined with good dating skills. Therefore, the rest of this chapter outlines skills that will boost your dating success. As you'll notice, many of these skills involve bringing more mindfulness to interactions with your date, allowing you to have a good time, connect with your positive emotions, and enjoy yourself. After all, dating someone you like is a very exhilarating and fun experience.

Ways to Engage with Your Date

Have you ever noticed that in the movies dates tend to go off without a hitch, with even awkward moments ending up endearing and cute? Despite these skewed portrayals, there's actually no perfect way to act or be on a date. Awkward silences, starting to talk at the same time, spilling your drink, dropping your phone, running into an ex, saying too much, saying too little—all of these things and more happen on normal dates. Fortunately, the most important factor for successful dating isn't avoiding social mishaps or having a perfectly smooth date. (Whew—huge sigh of relief!) The key is engaging with each other in a genuine way.

Engaging in this way has to do with responding to who the other person is and being genuine in what that person brings out in you. This is worlds apart from developing rehearsed lines to try to get girls or make guys fall for you, and it works because everyone is different and every couple's interactions are different. That's part of the beauty of finding someone you hit it off with, and it's exciting.

Although there's no formula for having a great connection with anyone you date, you can learn skills that will increase your chances of connecting. And if the precursors for compatibility are there, meaning you share similar values or ways of seeing the world, the way you engage with your date can make the connection even more successful.

Of course, mindfulness can enhance a variety of relationship skills: listening, sharing, responding empathetically, employing humor, disclosing about yourself, being authentic, and even knowing when to let a relationship go. In addition, engagement is something that works both ways. How someone listens tells you a lot of about the type of partner that person would be, just as how you listen and communicate tells others about the type of partner you'd be. Forming a relationship is about getting to know each other and building trust and intimacy, both physically and emotionally. It's also about setting the stage for your relationship. Mindful attention can not only help you connect with someone great, but also help you determine who will be a good long-term partner.

Being Authentic and Genuine

People who have happy romantic relationships are able to confide and seek comfort in one another (Mikulincer and Shaver 2007).

They're also able to be friends and have a blast together. In order to do all of those things, you have to be able to let your guard down and be genuine with your partner.

Dating is often a way to get to know others to discover if you want to be in a relationship with them. Therefore, it's crucial that you feel you can be yourself around people you're attracted to. It might be tempting to try to act the way you think they'd like you to or answer questions how you think they want you to. But if you feel you have to behave in certain ways or say certain things to get someone to like you, that puts a potential relationship on a shaky foundation from the get-go. In the long run, you're likely to disappoint or confuse the other person when you begin acting more authentically, or you'll have to keep up a facade, which is a hard way to live and prevents true intimacy.

This doesn't mean you shouldn't put your best foot forward. It doesn't mean that you should tell your date your worst fears or biggest flaws on the first date—or even the second or third. And I'm not saying you shouldn't be especially polite or considerate. Ultimately, the general way you act and react around your date should feel like one that wouldn't surprise your close friends if they were to overhear the conversation.

Engaging Through Humor and Playfulness

It's natural to be attracted to people who are lighthearted and can see the fun side to life. And especially in the early stages of a relationship, it can be really nice to focus on simply having fun with your date. It takes the pressure off of both of you. Ask yourself, *Is this someone I'd want to go to a theme park with? Is this someone who can put a smile on my face?* After all, if you might be interested in spending a lifetime with someone, you probably want to be able to have fun with that person. While humor is important to everyone, some studies indicate that men and women are drawn to slightly different aspects of humor in dating: men tend to be drawn to women who laugh at their jokes, while women tend to prefer a man who will make them laugh (Bressler, Martin, and

Balshine 2006). Being mindful on your dates allows you to take advantage of moments when humor and lightheartedness enter the conversation or interaction.

One of the great things about being genuine is that it allows you to find someone whose sense of humor is similar to yours. This can set the stage for developing ongoing or inside jokes between the two of you, increasing your sense of compatibility.

Approaching each date with the intention to be in the moment, have fun, and truly experience the other person can help you remember to bring some playfulness to it. You might repeat a mantra to help you keep this intention in mind, such as "It's not about being perfect; it's about having fun together."

Being an Attentive Listener

When you're having a conversation with someone on a date, what are you usually focused on? Is it the content of what the other person is saying? Or are you thinking about how you'll respond and trying to figure out the "right" thing to say?

Social anxiety can make it tough to be present in conversations because it tends to create a compelling running dialogue in your mind, analyzing and evaluating what you just said, how you should respond, and whether you should share what's on your mind. You can counteract this tendency by bringing mindfulness to the conversation and focusing on what your date is saying. Really hear the other person's words and tune in to the meaning.

Consider Scott, who went out on a first date with Heidi. After Heidi mentioned that she was a journalist, she said, "I really like my work. I never thought I'd end up in this field, but it's been better than I ever imagined."

Scott replied, "That's great. My work is pretty good, too. I mean, I sort of had to go into the family business because of my dad, but it's worked out. I make a good living."

While there's nothing wrong with Scott's response, he missed an opportunity to engage with Heidi by listening attentively and then responding more directly to what she was talking about. Instead, he followed an agenda of telling Heidi about his career because he thought she'd be attracted to the idea that he had a solid career and earned well. Because his focus was on how Heidi would perceive him, he didn't take the opportunity to learn more about her work. There are so many questions he might have asked: "What is it about your work that you enjoy so much?" "Why didn't you think you'd ever get into that line of work?" "How is it better than you imagined?" These kinds of responses would show that he was really listening to Heidi and curious about her experiences, rather than bringing the conversation back to himself.

When you're in the moment and engaged in a conversation, active listening skills will help you connect with what your date is saying and stay with that topic. Some of the best ways to engage in active listening include asking questions, responding empathetically, and responding with personal disclosure when appropriate.

Asking Questions

Asking your date to tell you more about what she's talking about shows that you're attentive and is also an indication of your ability to care about someone else. Of course, it's important to be authentic, so the questions you ask should reflect your genuine interest. What did the other person say that made you curious to know more?

To practice asking attentive questions, work on this skill in your everyday life, whether with colleagues, friends, casual acquaintances, or dates. Notice what it feels like to pay attention to others' responses, and also notice how they respond to being asked for more information. People usually respond in a very positive way because they feel their perspective is appreciated. Here are some types of questions you might use:

- ➥ **Inquiry for their expertise:** Ask others to tell you more about how they did something or how something works in their area of expertise. For instance, Scott could ask Heidi about how she got into journalism and what it's like to work on a deadline.

↪ **Inquiry about their experience:** Asking about others' experience is extremely helpful in getting to know them. For instance, Scott could ask Heidi what it was like the first time she interviewed a convicted criminal or which news stories she felt most passionate about. This would help him get to know her personality and would also show an interest in her feelings.

↪ **Inquiry about the future:** Another type of question to ask is about others' hopes or dreams for the future. For example, Scott might ask Heidi what her ideal story would be, or whether she ever envisions changing careers at some point. These kinds of questions help you bond to a love interest, in part because it's exciting to think about the possibilities in life, and because it can suggest that the two of you will still be in each other's lives in the future.

Responding Empathetically

Think back to a time when you felt someone was really listening to you, a time when you felt truly understood and heard. Maybe it was a close friend or mentor, or perhaps it was a parent or sibling. Being heard and knowing that the other person understands is a powerful experience. It indicates that the other person has empathy—that she can put herself in your shoes and imagine what you're going through.

Responding to your date with empathy will certainly help you connect with her. After all, everyone wants to be with someone who really gets them. For instance, my client Brayden was telling Claudia about his college job as a ski instructor each winter, animatedly talking about how those were his fondest memories from his college days. She responded, "That must have been so fun for you to do every year! It sounds like such a unique experience." This was an empathetic response because it showed that Claudia could imagine and understand how Brayden felt about that job and that time in his life. Similarly, Sonya was telling her date, Manuel, about her roommate eloping the previous summer and leaving without any notice or paying her rent. When Manuel replied, "That must have been stressful for you," she felt like he understood where she was coming from.

The key to empathy is listening to what the other person is telling you and paying attention to the emotions he seems to be feeling. If a date is talking fondly about his dog, Scruffy, and showing you a picture of the dog, an empathetic response might be, "It seems like you really love your dog." If your date is talking about how he can't believe the Giants lost to the Eagles, an empathetic response might be, "I can tell you're passionate about your team."

However, there is one caveat: I've noticed that people who are shy or anxious sometimes ask questions and respond empathetically so they won't have to talk about themselves. Keep in mind that sharing your own thoughts and feelings and speaking openly is the other side of the equation in actively engaging with your date.

Offering Personal Disclosure

Personal disclosure means sharing information about yourself, and particularly your thoughts and feelings. In the context of dating, attentive listening, and active engagement, it means sharing how you were affected by what the other person said. For instance, if your date tells you about an aspect of his life that impresses you, perhaps a volunteer trip he took last summer, you might disclose your feelings by saying, "Wow, that's really amazing! I don't think any experience can affect you or change you as much as being in a new environment like that. Traveling has really changed my perspective. Those are some of my best memories. I think it's really cool that you did that." Likewise, if your date tells you that she hates it when people take photos of their food before they eat to post it to Instagram, you can say, "I know! I've never understood the fascination with that. I appreciate a good meal, but it just wouldn't occur to me that anyone else would be interested in my lunch."

The purpose of personal disclosure is to genuinely show how you relate to what your date is saying. If something she says makes you laugh, tell her you think it's funny. If you disagree with something he says, tell him you have a different take on it. If she tells a story that you think is sweet, let her know. If you're excited by an idea he has, tell him how cool you think it is. When you're able to genuinely convey how your date's words are affecting you, it creates a more lively dynamic between the two of you.

One common reason why people don't offer personal disclosure is fear of rejection. Hopefully some of the exercises in chapter 2 have helped you learn to deal with fear of rejection. When you extend mindful acceptance to this fear, you'll notice that it no longer holds you back from sharing your thoughts, especially when you're with someone you feel connected to. Among my clients who are smart and successful, it's also common to worry that their dates will find them intimidating if they share their thoughts and opinions. They worry about coming off as full of themselves. However, being genuine and sharing your intelligence and insight will only serve to attract the right person to you.

Alternatively, sometimes shy people hesitate to offer self-disclosure because they're worried about oversharing. If you're feeling a strong connection with someone and starting to let your guard down, you might wonder how much to disclose about yourself, and especially about your struggles. Do you tell your date about the extent of your dating anxiety? Do you mention that you've always been shy? Mindfulness can be helpful in navigating this issue. Tuning in during your conversations will help you monitor how much you're disclosing about yourself and how the other person is responding. When you're grounded in the present moment, you're less likely to get lost in telling your date about something you might later regret. It helps you think about what you're sharing and also helps you listen to your instinct if you may be sharing too much.

Being Aware of a Tendency to Put Yourself Down

People who are socially anxious to tend to have lower self-esteem and make automatic negative assumptions about themselves (Glashouwer et al. 2013). For instance, Gretchen had heard a lot about her friend Sasha's cousin Quinn and wanted to meet him. When Sasha introduced them at a party, Quinn said, "Sasha says we have a lot in common. She always speaks very highly of you. She told me what a great teacher you are and how all the kids love you. I've been looking forward to meeting you." Gretchen automatically worried that she wasn't as good as Sasha had made her out to be and became very uncomfortable. She usually felt incompetent at work, despite receiving a lot of positive feedback, which she tended to dismiss. She told Quinn, "Well, Sasha is a good friend. She speaks highly of everyone, and she probably exaggerated. I hope I don't disappoint you." Gretchen had trouble receiving the compliment that Quinn had been looking forward to meeting her.

These kinds of automatic negative feelings and reactions interfere with active, genuine engagement. Mindfulness of your reactions can be helpful here. If you notice that you're having a strong reaction to hearing a compliment or receiving attention, you can decide how you wish to respond. Then, instead of rejecting compliments or deflecting attention, you might choose to be more open to receiving praise. Perhaps you'd want to respond with a simple thank-you or return the compliment. In this way, mindfulness allows for more flexibility in your responses.

Being Open to Noticing the Positives

With social anxiety and shyness, there's also tendency to filter out some of the positive aspects of your experience and interactions and focus on the negatives. Like rejecting compliments, this response can be automatic, so it may be hard to notice that you're focusing on nega-tives. This is another great target for mindfulness. As an added incen-tive, research has shown that people who are optimistic and positive tend to cope with stress more easily than those who are pessimistic (Jobin, Wrosch, and Scheier 2013). So you may find it helpful to think about being positive as a way to help you de-stress and engage with your date.

Tune in to the positives, including your date's positive traits. Then affirm these positives with your behavior. This might include giving your date a compliment, such as telling him he picked a great restau-rant. Or it might mean sharing an upbeat story, perhaps telling your date about a happy incident earlier in your day. Likewise, find moments or things that you appreciate during your date and share these with the other person. Perhaps you like the fact that she was on time, appreciate that he holds the door for you, or love the view while you're walking together. People like being around people who appreciate them and take the time to point out the positives.

Being Open to Flirtation

In much this same way, it's helpful to be open to flirting and showing that you like your date when things are going well. You might notice that you have a lot in common and are enjoying your time together and decide to raise your glass: "Cheers to having dinner with a beautiful woman, and cheers to a wonderful evening together." Flirting is all about being in the moment and allowing yourself to savor the pleasure and excitement of being attracted to someone. Don't worry that flirting will drive the other person away. If anything, knowing that you are indeed interested will help your date feel more secure and con-fident. Whether it's giving him a subtle smile, whispering something sweet to her in a playful manner, placing your hand gently on his shoul-der, or a sitting close together side-by-side, flirting can be one of the most enjoyable parts of dating.

Knowing When to Stick With It

While dating will undoubtedly bring out some anxiety, the deepening of a new relationship can do the same. If you're afraid of being hurt or getting too close to someone who might ultimately reject you, you may have an urge to flee. As a result, you might distance yourself in smaller ways, like not returning phone calls, or you might end the relationship. You could find yourself in a pattern of consistently withdrawing from each person you date, effectively sabotaging your relationships out of fear of intimacy. Avoiding a deeper relationship allows you to avoid anxiety, but it prevents you from forming the close relationships you probably desire.

Consider your past experiences in dating or relationships: Have you ever let yourself truly get close to someone, or have you kept your guard up or used anxiety as a defense against getting close? Take some time to consider both the risks and the rewards of getting close to someone. It's true that there are no guarantees that you won't get hurt, but at some point, with the right person, you may want to risk being vulnerable, or becoming vulnerable again if you've been hurt in the past. You need to be willing to tolerate anxiety about the unknown if you are to enjoy the benefits and excitement of a good relationship.

If you're starting to develop a new relationship that you want to pursue but feel a pull to withdraw, challenge yourself to work through the anxiety. Allow yourself to continue spending time with the person while tuning in to your emotions. While you may have a strong urge to withdraw due to intimacy-related anxiety, the skill of staying in the moment and with the anxiety will ultimately serve you well in determining how you truly feel about someone.

Knowing When to Let It Go

On the other hand, some people react to anxiety not by withdrawing, but by seeking attachment to a someone who isn't a good fit for them or doesn't reciprocate their feelings. This can be another way of avoiding true intimacy. My clients often talk about people they're dating with a focus on whether the other person likes them, how to get the other person to like them more, or how to be more attractive to the other person. This is understandable; it's natural to want to be liked and accepted, particularly for people who struggle with self-doubt and low self-esteem. But sometimes getting caught up in wanting to be liked detracts from the equally important issue of deciding whether the other person is someone you want to be with. Don't overlook the crucial question of whether you want to see a particular person again. Anxiety can make you ignore red flags in relationships if you aren't self-aware.

Paying attention to your interactions and your reactions to them can tell you a lot. For instance, my client Ella had been out with Leo a few times. He seemed charming, attentive, and smart at first, but after a few dates she noticed that she always felt like he was being critical of her. Initially, she thought she was just projecting her insecurity onto him, so she assumed her feelings weren't an accurate reflection of Leo. But the nagging feeling that something wasn't right continued.

When Ella came to session, she told me that Leo didn't seem very affectionate and attentive, and she wondered how she could make him like her more or treat her better. I shifted the focus away from how much or little Leo liked her and brought it to how Ella felt around him. As she paid attention to these feelings, Ella started to notice that it wasn't just her insecurity: Leo really was subtly putting her down. He tended to minimize her career and friendships, which were both really important to her. He also made all of the decisions about their dates, and although she found that attractive at first, it eventually became stifling. Ella realized that she felt less secure and confident around Leo. Being open to her experience and in touch with her instincts helped Ella make the decision to stop seeing him before she invested more into the relationship.

Being attuned to your experience can help you notice whether things are going well and when it might be time to leave. Don't be afraid to trust your instincts. Instincts are different than urges. Whereas urges occur as a reaction to anxiety, instincts (in this case, about dating) are natural feelings you get when you consider the relationship as a whole.

While feeling comfortable and self-confident around someone new can take time, there are certain indicators that a person may not be good relationship material: being argumentative or disrespectful, being late on a regular basis, making jokes at your expense, expecting you to pay for everything, calling at the last minute or infrequently, or ignoring your calls. It's best to let these people go, even if it means being single a bit longer, rather than to settle and then spend months or years feeling discontent or trying to change your partner. Don't be afraid to end it. Someone better for you will come along.

Summary

In this chapter, you learned some introductory mindfulness skills and learned how practicing mindfulness can help you engage with others. Building on your dating skills, you've learned how authenticity, humor, good listening skills, empathy, and self-disclosure can help you forge a closer connection with your date. As you tune in to your emotions, you can also notice how your feelings tend to drive your behavior. This awareness paves the way for you to choose new alternatives to old, automatic reactions. You can begin to accept compliments, have fun, and enjoy the positives of dating. The accumulation of these skills helps you build a strong foundation in potential new relationships. It can also help you evaluate when it's time to cut your losses and move on—a key skill for dating success.

In the next chapter, I'll help you explore and discover—or rediscover—the areas you really care about in life and the type of partner who might be a good fit for you. Finding your true desires and passions in life, clarifying your values, and taking control of your life direction and decisions will help you to find a relationship where you can be authentically you within—and beyond—your dating relationships.

CHAPTER 5

---- ➤ ♥ ◄ ----

What Really Matters to You in Life and in a Relationship

My client Jonah was a twenty-nine-year-old CPA. After several years working at an accounting firm, putting in long hours and receiving several promotions, Jonah noticed a growing sense of emptiness. He hadn't dated much and justified his lack of a love life by telling himself work was his top priority and that he'd meet someone eventually. But the truth was, he was worried that he didn't have a lot to offer, and it made him uncomfortable to ask women out or be set up. And the older he got, the more difficult it became to meet new people. Meanwhile, most of his friends had gotten married, and many of them had kids.

At the wedding of his childhood best friend, where he served as groomsman, Jonah started giving some deep thought to his own life purpose and path. He realized that he'd gotten stuck in a routine that facilitated his career and not much else. Most days he worked late, and by the time he got home, he didn't have time or energy for anything other than a quick dinner and maybe a jog before hitting the sack. He no longer had a sense of meaning or joy in life, and he worried that life was passing him by. Toasting the groom at his best friend's wedding, whom he truly wished all the happiness in the world, he couldn't help but feel empty and a little lonely.

In therapy, he contemplated what was missing and how he'd gotten to this point. He realized that when he was growing up, his parents had given him the impression that the key to happiness was financial stability. And indeed, having a solid career was important to him and definitely added to his quality of life, but it wasn't enough. I helped him start thinking about ways to bring more meaning into his life and more diversity and richness to his routine.

Drawing on his fond memories of playing on the basketball team in high school, Jonah decided to join a weekend flag football team. He also made an effort to reconnect with his family. He started occasionally accepting his sister's standing offer to come over on weekends and also took his niece and nephew out for one-on-one time some weekends. Even though Jonah considered himself a fairly introverted guy, he noticed that he felt better when he saw his family or got together with friends at least once a week.

As a next step, Jonah began to date a little more. He recognized that he valued having a relationship even if asking women out caused him some anxiety. He went out with a few women who worked in his building, but none of the dates went well. He told me he felt awkward and as though he didn't have much in common with the women. He also went on a blind date with a friend of a friend, and it was filled with uncomfortable silences. He wondered why he was going through all of this effort only to end up feeling more miserable. We revisited his values around relationships and developing a more well-rounded life, and that bolstered his willingness to continue dating.

Then he met Hayley at a flag football league picnic. She seemed like such an interesting and attractive person. So despite his hesitation and an inner dialogue telling him it wouldn't work out, Jonah looked for opportunities to be around her more. He went to team parties and happy hours, which he normally would have opted out of, and eventually he asked her out. As he and Hayley started spending more time together, Jonah discovered that he loved how she brought out the liveliness in him. Around her he felt like himself, only better—more self-assured and caring somehow. He began to feel like he had a lot to offer.

Looking back, he saw that his focus on his career had been a way to avoid dealing with his shyness. And his dedication to his career had made him feel that it was okay if other areas of his life weren't a priority. But living his life in a way that was more balanced—and didn't consist solely of work—felt more rich and meaningful to him.

❣

There are all kinds of reasons why people get adrift in life, not pursuing what matters to them. First, like Jonah, many people fear the unknown and therefore stay inside their comfort zone, safe but unfulfilled. Also like Jonah, many people come to believe that financial success or career accomplishments are the best route to happiness and satisfaction, but this can get in the way of self-reflection and connection with others. And many people simply get swept up in the fast pace of life and don't take time out to reflect on their course and whether it's truly what they want.

Next, anxiety and shyness can also be a factor, creating a focus on trying to avoid feeling anxious, embarrassed, or bad. You may not even think about what you're missing out on. Or perhaps you go into problem-solving mode, becoming preoccupied with reviewing how anxiety might show up in the future and how to avoid that anxiety. But this effort to avoid upsetting emotions causes your life to revolve around figuring out how you can avoid negative experiences, such as shame or embarrassment, rather than figuring out how to get what you do want, such as a rich social life or a fulfilling relationship. You may entirely abandon your values and aspirations in an effort to avoid uncomfortable experiences. Being anxiety-free starts to seem like the ultimate goal in life.

Lastly, you may sabotage yourself with thoughts like *If only I didn't have this anxiety, life would be good.* This can start to make life seem black-and-white: you're either happy or anxious, content or discontent. It becomes all too easy to lose sight of subtle nuances and underestimate the complexity of life.

Mindfulness allows you to appreciate the richness of life as you experience it. There's freedom in recognizing that some suffering is a normal part of life. Adversity, struggle, and difficulty are just a part of the package deal that comes with living, dating, falling in love, and being in a relationship. In the end, the challenges are worthwhile because they allow you to develop meaningful relationships.

Living a Valued Life

One of the primary themes of ACT is living in a way that's in line with your core values. The goal of this chapter is to help you get in touch with what you most deeply care about. It also examines the ingredients that are crucial to happy and successful relationships. I'll discuss problematic choices that anxious people may make regarding partners and take a look at how to instead identify people who are likely to be compatible with you long-term.

This chapter will help you explore what inspires you, makes you feel most alive, and brings you the deepest feelings of contentment. It will help you start living in greater alignment with your values, rather than in the shadow of anxiety. It will help you see that the moments in life when you feel most alive are almost always complex, filled with sweetness and also tinges of sorrow or distress. Embracing this complexity in life will allow you to strengthen your connection with yourself.

By clarifying your values with the exercises in this chapter, you'll move toward living your life in a way that's more congruent with those values. Making small everyday choices that align with your values adds up. With time, this helps you live more fully, rather than simply existing, and helps you take full advantage of your life's potential. Research has shown that connecting to larger values and a purpose in life leads to more positive emotions, higher self-esteem, and a sense of deeper meaning in life on the days when people are most aligned with their values and interests (Hayes et al. 2006). Ultimately, clarifying your values can help you find a purpose in life, and people who live with a sense of purpose tend to have higher levels of well-being (McKnight and Kashdan 2009).

Another benefit to values clarification is that it can help you make key partner decisions in life. Holding similar values (Archuleta 2013), being supportive of one another, and having a strong emotional connection (Schröder-Abé and Schütz 2011) are the qualities that enduring, loving relationships are made of. When you know yourself, it helps you make good choices about who you date. You also strengthen your sense of inner contentment, creating a solid foundation that will serve you well when entering into new relationships. In addition, it can help you find a partner who truly suits you by narrowing down qualities that are important to you in a partner.

Finding someone with values similar to yours might initially feel like a tall order. You may think, *I have trouble meeting anyone, let alone someone who has similar values.* This is one reason why people who are shy or anxious may find it tempting to go out with the first person who pursues them. I've seen example after example of shy people ending up in unfulfilling relationships. When they look back, they can see that they began the relationship because the other person showed interest, was attractive, or was the first person with whom they didn't feel shy or anxious. Again, these aren't necessarily the ingredients for a happy relationship.

In fact, it might be a bit of a red flag if a partner doesn't make you feel anxious. Maybe he doesn't make you nervous because he doesn't excite or challenge you. Maybe she feels safe but not special. If you realize that you ended up with someone because that person chose you and pursued you, you may wonder, *Did I choose this person, or am I in this relationship because I went along with the first person who pursued me?*

Research indicates that people who fear being single often end up settling for less in their relationships (Spielmann et al. 2013). Struggling with shyness and anxiety can exacerbate this fear of being single. But settling for someone who doesn't really hold the qualities you desire isn't the only choice you have. Regardless of whether you are shy or anxious, setting your sights on finding a compatible partner who can enhance your life is crucial to your satisfaction.

A final issue is that people with shyness and social anxiety tend to have more trouble identifying, experiencing, and embracing positive moments and emotions in life (Kashdan, Weeks, and Savostyanova 2011). Further, they typically try to suppress most emotional experiences. This creates a vicious cycle, as a lack of positive experiences and positive emotions can increase shyness and anxiety. Connecting to your values is an effective way to recognize, appreciate, and savor the good moments when they occur. This, in turn, can enhance your ability to connect to others in a positive, meaningful way.

This chapter will walk you through the process of identifying people who might be a good fit for you. First you'll explore and define your own values, and then you'll look at the values you'd like in a partner. Then, as you date various people, you can begin to determine who could be a truly good choice for you based on qualities that might enhance the long-term success of the relationship.

———➡ **Exercise:** Finding the Sweet Spot

This exercise (reprinted with permission from Wilson and Sandoz 2008) will help you begin to think about your values in a new way. Rather than zeroing in on words that define your values, it helps you focus on the experiences and feelings associated with those values and see how values translate into real-life experiences. It will also help you define what you value by exploring a good moment in your life.

Life comes with many struggles, anxieties, and insecurities. But this exercise is going to focus on finding a moment in which you've found sweetness in your life. To begin, sit comfortably with your feet on the ground and your hands at your sides or in your lap. Gently close your eyes.

Call to mind a moment when you felt really alive, when the struggle that has had its grip on you just fell away for a moment—a moment completely without effort, when you knew who you were, and where you belonged. It could be something recent or something long past.... Call to mind just one. It doesn't have to be the most important or the happiest moment. It may be something really simple. You may even find a little bit of sadness there. See if you can just let that be there for just a moment. Just allow yourself to drift back into that moment and just be there briefly, in that moment of sweetness.

Once you've found a sweet spot, stay in it for a little while. Then gently open your eyes. In your journal, write down a few of the images, words, or feelings that came to mind while you were in that spot. You don't have to describe exactly what happened or where you were; instead, focus on capturing the key elements of what that moment of your life was like. Take your time, savoring the exercise and slowing down to notice each feeling and image. There are nuances you might see—things you might miss if you hurry or don't take the time to write about them. So in the gentlest way you can, let yourself express that sweet moment.

⟶ **Exercise:** Heightening the Sweet Spot

The next exercise (also reprinted with permission from Wilson and Sandoz 2008) is focused on further exploring the sensations, perceptions, and ingredients that created your experience of a sweet spot. It will take just a dash of fantasy as you allow yourself to travel back, perhaps calling on that childhood ability to defy time and gravity through your imagination. Once again, sit comfortably with your feet on the ground and your hands at your sides or in your lap, then gently close your eyes.

If you could imagine that you have a sort of checklist, I'd like you to just notice, beginning with the most prominent sounds, just notice them and imagine that you check them off the list. See if you can listen for smaller, more subtle sounds. You might hear the sounds of vehicles outside, the murmur of people speaking in other rooms. And breathe. Begin to draw your attention to your own body. Begin to notice places where your body makes contact with the floor and the chair. And, breathe. Notice especially the little places where you can feel the transition in that contact. Notice the very edges of the place on your back that are touching the chair. See if in your mind's eye you can trace that margin. See if you can begin to notice the smallest details in sensation that tell you this part is touching and that is not. And, breathe.

Now, I'd like you to imagine that in front of you there is a file cabinet. In the file cabinet let there be photographs. Imagine that you open the drawer and reach in and withdraw a picture of you during that sweet moment. And, if there is not a picture there, just let one materialize. Let yourself draw that picture up from the file cabinet and feel it in your hands. Let yourself notice the sensations in your fingertips as you gently hold the photo. Let yourself look into that face of yours in that picture and let yourself notice the details surrounding you. Let yourself see your own face—the cut of your hair, the set of your jaw, the look in your eyes.

And now, I want you to imagine that your awareness is some sort of liquid that could be poured into that you in that picture. So, imagine that your awareness is beginning to pour into the skin of that you in that very moment. Let yourself see what you see there. Let yourself notice the sensations that you feel on your own skin in that sweet place. If you are outdoors perhaps you feel a slight breeze. If you're with someone you might feel the warmth of their skin against you, the scent of their hair. Let it be as if you could just breathe that moment in and out. Let yourself feel the life in that moment. As if each breath filled you with that sweetness. Let it be as if every cell in your body can feel what it is to be in that place. Just take a moment to luxuriate in that presence.

When you're ready, allow yourself to hold gratitude for that moment. Then gently open your eyes and allow yourself to return, feeling renewed and inspired because of having been to that sweet place. You may want to take a few minutes to reflect on your experience in your journal:

- What did it feel like to see yourself in that photo? Did you have a sense of wanting to connect more with the you who you saw in that scene?

- What do you think it was about this sweet spot that resonated with you? What memories, sounds, or emotions were most poignant?

- Can you identify other experiences that were also sweet spots? Perhaps you'll recall a positive interaction with someone or receiving a compliment. Keeping a list of your sweet spots can help you practice connecting to positive moments in your past, paving the way for more sweet spots to come.

This exercise is particularly helpful for shyness and anxiety because it helps you move away from judging yourself and downplaying your positive experiences. Instead, you approach life from a place of willingness—willingness to feel your feelings as they come, to accept the moment as it is, and to feel the vitality in life.

⟶ **Exercise:** Exploring Your Values

Connecting with your sweet spot puts you directly in touch with your values at a very deep emotional level. Having established that connection, you're now in a good position to begin exploring your values more specifically. Withdrawal, avoidance, and fear of being judged—all hallmarks of shyness and social anxiety—may have prevented you from considering your values or living in alignment with them. In this exercise, you'll consider what you hold most dear in life and what you most care about regarding the people and events in your life. You'll want to keep your answers in mind, because in chapter 6 you'll focus on implementing these values into your daily routine.

Take some time to consider the following questions, then write your responses in your journal:

- Recall the last time you felt proud of yourself. What was it about your accomplishment that felt satisfying?

- What do you most admire or envy in others?

- Think about the last time you were deeply affected by someone in a positive way. What did the other person say or do to affect you in that way? What values do you associate with the other person's behavior?

- If you had only one year left to live, how would want you spend your time, and with whom? What would you no longer concern yourself with?

- If you could accomplish anything in the next year, with no limits or boundaries at all, what would you want to do?

- Is there anything you believe in deeply? What is it, and what helps you hold that conviction?

Being naturally shy and anxious leaves you susceptible to living according to others' values. This is because you may fear that others will think poorly of you if you don't act according to what they value. This can be true of interactions with your family, colleagues or superiors at work, and friends, and also with dating partners. Take some time now to consider values that may have been imposed on you by others:

- Growing up, did you learn that you should hold certain values?

- How did you feel if you didn't uphold those values? How did others treat you if you didn't uphold those values? Did you receive reprimands or feel that others were disappointed? Did you feel guilty?

- Are there certain values you feel you should hold but that don't resonate with you deeply? Do you ever feel pressure to conform to how others want you to be?

- What do you think others expect from you in dating or love relationships?

These are all key questions to consider, especially if you're anxious. You may put pressure on yourself to please others and meet expectations you think they have for you. This can be a barrier to being clear about your own values. Identifying what you believe and care about is an important part of being authentic and developing relationships that work well for you.

Shyness, Passivity, and Values

In the past, being shy may have prevented you from fully exploring your values. Shyness can cause you to take a more passive role in your own life, waiting for things to happen to you and assuming that your role is to take what life gives you. In this scenario, it can seem as though your values aren't an important factor in what you can expect from life, so you may not give yourself the opportunity to strive for what you really want.

Passivity means that your mode of making decisions is actually to *not* make decisions. For instance, say you attend a singles mixer, don't speak to anyone, and then leave after a half hour. If someone were to ask you whether you met anyone new, you might naturally reply, "No. No one talked to me." But talking to someone isn't just about waiting for someone to come to you. You also decide whether you'll approach others to talk to them. So the experience "No one talked to me" is only partially true.

This is actually good news. Once you're aware that passivity is indeed a choice, you can start to be more mindful of when and where you're making the choice to be passive. Then you can connect with your values, decide whether you want to interact, and then call up the willingness to do so. This puts you more in control of your end of the equation in any social situation. You can choose passivity, or you can choose to be active.

The decisions you make—whether to go out, who to go out with, whether you choose to spend an evening home alone, and so on—all affect your future. Life is a series of small decisions, and you're the one in control of how your respond to your options. The question is, do you want to make your decisions passively, based on avoidance, shyness, and maintaining the status quo, or do you want to actively make your decisions based on your values and inner desires?

You're probably reading this book because you feel discontented or have a sense that you're not living the life you want. In part, this may be because you've been basing decisions on shyness or anxiety and some amount of passivity. Basing decisions on anxiety or passivity often gets you more of the same. While it is your choice to make, my guess is that since you're reading this book, you're ready for change. To get on a different track, you'll need to start basing your decisions on a different set of criteria: your values and authentic desires.

──➤ **Exercise:** Creating a Values Inventory

This exercise (inspired in part by Hayes 2005) will help you clarify your values. It will also help you see the ways in which you're already living by your values and identify areas you want to focus on in dating, finding a partner, and building a relationship.

An essential component of ACT is examining values in different domains of life. Studies show that shy and anxious people who participate in ACT—including values clarification in various domains of life—have greater perceived quality of life and fewer symptoms of social anxiety (Dalyrmple and Herbert 2007). These benefits can help you overcome the barriers that shyness and social anxiety can present in dating and love.

Having a well-rounded life is such an important aspect of finding love. Many of my clients have found that when they devote the time and energy to enriching other areas of their life, they feel better about themselves and what they have to offer a partner. Their sense of balance and passion for life, along with their clear sense of self, is appealing to potential partners. They also feel that being clear about their values helps them choose potential partners who are on the same page.

Considering your values in various domains will help you choose a partner who you're compatible with. Many of the people I work with in couples therapy have fundamentally different views in some life domains, and this can make it harder for a relationship to work unless you've talked through these differences and how you'll handle them. By looking at these domains now, you're making a preemptive move on potential future trouble spots.

Give some thought to each of the domains outlined below, then answer the questions about each in your journal. There are no right or wrong answers to any of these questions. Some domains will resonate deeply with you. Other areas may not apply to you, and that's okay. What's important is that you establish a strong base from which to build a life that feels full of purpose and is heading in the direction you want to go.

Intimate Relationship

Intimate relationships are at the heart of this book, so they're a good place to begin this inventory. We'll explore this domain in greater detail toward the end of the chapter. Here, you'll start by considering some key elements of your values relating to dating and intimate relationships.

- What is your ideal level of commitment?

- What traits do you value in marriage or a partnership?

- Write down some key words or qualities that describe your values regarding a fulfilling relationship.

- How important is it to you that a partner share your values in this domain?

Friendship

Friendship has to do with camaraderie, mutual support, enjoying activities together, and sharing humor and confidences.

- Ask yourself what friendships, current or past, have been the most significant to you and why.

- Is friendship an area in your life that you value and want to spend more time on, either reconnecting with old friends or pursuing new friendships?

- Is there a way in which your friendships might be holding you back in life?

- How would you like this domain to be present in an intimate relationship? Is it important that your friends get along with your partner? How important is it that you like your partner's friends? Do you want to socialize with others together? Do you want to make time for your friendships outside of your relationship?

- How important is it to you that a partner share your values in this domain?

Family

Family is defined by your nuclear and extended family.

- Ask yourself what family relationships have been the most meaningful to you. When were these relationships the closest?

- What do you believe brings people closer or creates distance in a family?

- What values do you hold regarding family relationships?

- How important is it to you that a partner share your values in this domain?

Work and Education

Your work is how you earn a living and where you probably spend a lot of your time. Some people find their work intrinsically meaningful, while others value what work provides for them, such as money and the ability to support a family. Education has to do with gaining knowledge about a particular topic and includes obtaining a degree from a formal institution, learning on your own through reading or research, or continuing to seek out environments where you expand your frame of reference. If you aren't currently working, you can explore this domain by considering what would be important to you in a future career.

- What areas of your career or occupation do you value?

- What values played a role in your decision to choose this career path?

- What's your perspective on work ethic? Which values are important to you in the workplace?

- What values do you hold regarding education? How has it affected who you are? What role might education play in your future?

- How important is it to you that a partner share your values in this domain?

Parenting

The domain of parenting is about your beliefs and values surrounding having children, including whether or not you want to have children.

- If you're a parent, ask yourself what you value about your role as a parent. What do you value in a partner in regard to your kids? How would you like a partner to be involved in your kids' lives?

- If you're not a parent, what are your views on parenthood? What are your reasons for wanting to have kids or not have kids?

- How would you like this domain to be present in an intimate relationship?

- How important is it to you that a partner share your values in this domain?

Recreation

Recreation is leisure, fun, play, sport, or activities enjoyed outside of working hours.

- What are your values around leisure and recreation? Do you highly value free time, or does too much free time leave you uneasy?

- If you had a day completely free of responsibilities, and with no limits, what would you do?

- Consider how you spend most of your free time. Is there a disparity in what you'd ideally be doing in your spare time and what you're actually doing in your spare time?

- How would you like this domain to be present in an intimate relationship? Do you wish to spend your leisure time separately, together, or together just sometimes?

- How important is it to you that a partner share your values in this domain?

Spirituality

Spirituality is your relationship with a higher power or organized religion. People often find that their spirituality is what helps them understand their own existence and purpose for being alive. Consider what spirituality means for you.

- Is spirituality something you've longed for, something you currently feel connected with, or an area you aren't particularly interested in?

- While you were growing up, what experiences affected your view of spirituality?

- Are there moments when you've felt spiritually connected? How did those moments affect you?

- What role would you like spirituality to play in your intimate relationship?

- How important is it to you that a partner share your values in this domain?

Health and Wellness

The domain of health and wellness has to do with values surrounding physical fitness, food and alcohol intake, and self-care.

- What role does health and wellness play in your life?

- What is your current regimen related to physical fitness? Are there areas of this domain you'd like to change, and if so, what would you change?

- What are your feelings surrounding food? What about alcohol?

- How important is it to you that a partner share your values in this domain?

Values Unique to You

You may also hold unique values that don't fit into any of the categories above. Some people value cleanliness and a peaceful home environment. Perhaps you value creativity, imagination, or being artistic. Maybe you value your love of reading and getting lost in a good book. Perhaps you value saving money and being financially stable and secure. You could value your sense of fashion, your ability to coordinate a camping trip, your love of travel and adventure, or the peaceful feeling that comes with watching a sunset over the ocean. It could be your dedication, hard work, and perseverance through difficult periods, or it might be your ability to be playful and at ease with children. Perhaps it's your leadership ability, your knack for inspiring others to do great things, or your ability to foster teamwork by making everyone feel valued and included. There are so many aspects of life that can be important to your values system.

Take a few moments to think about other aspects of your life where you hold unique values, then write about this in your journal. Consider how you'd like these aspects of life to be present in an intimate relationship. Is it important to you that your partner hold similar values, or that your partner respect and encourage these attributes in you?

Partner Preferences

As you consider your own attributes, it will become easier to identify the values you'd like your partner to possess. Then, when dating, you can see how a person's values are reflected in various actions. Is she considerate of others when she speaks to them? Does he treat others well? Does she seem to have meaning in her life? Is he able to express care for the people in his life? What does she seem to value most in her life? Does he seem to like and accept who he is? All of these factors can inform your decisions about whether a potential partner holds values that blend well with yours.

Meeting someone can happen very quickly. You can go from being single to being in a relationship in just a few weeks—it only takes one person. Rather than waiting until you meet someone you really like to consider the characteristics you want in a partner, start asking yourself these questions now. Considering these important factors will help you approach dating with a clearer sense of what you want from a partner, setting the stage for seeking out those types of people.

The extent to which someone fits with your concept of an ideal partner can affect how satisfied you are with the relationship (Fletcher et al. 1999). Recently, researchers followed newlyweds for three and a half years, examining how their ideal partner traits matched up with the traits they actually saw in their partners and how this correlated to divorce rates (Eastwick and Neff 2012). They found that people were more likely to stay married when their perception of their spouse's traits matched their pattern of ideal partner preferences. In other words, believing your partner possesses the traits you find ideal makes it more likely your relationship will survive. Therefore, it's important to find a partner who generally fits with what you're looking for.

⟶ **Exercise:** Creating Your Relationship Inventory

This exercise will help you assess which traits you value in a partner or in a relationship. This knowledge will increase your chances of finding someone who's a good match for you.

- Write about the aspects of past dating partners or relationships that you've found fulfilling. Do you tend to like more introverted or more extroverted people? Do you need a lot of personal space, or do you like being very close and spending a great deal of time together?

Example: In my relationship with Melanie, I liked the way we laughed together and our mutual interest in cooking and exercising together. Melanie was more extroverted than I am, but it worked because she encouraged me to go out more and I influenced her to stay in for a cozy night at home sometimes.

- What aspects of your past relationships have been deal breakers for you? What are traits in a partner that you won't tolerate?

Example: Steve didn't get along with my family and didn't make an effort to get to know them. He was also immature, always joking about everything. We had a difficult time having serious conversations even when we really needed to talk. Traits I won't tolerate in a partner are bigotry, lack of motivation, and dependency.

- Think about couples whose relationship you admire and respect. For each couple, write their names and list aspects of their relationship that make them a strong couple or individual traits that have a positive effect on their relationship.

Example: Ellie and James. Caring, considerate, cooperative, fun, active, affectionate. Ellie and James approach things as a team. They seem to really love and adore each other, and they do a good job with their kids. Ellie is great at staying calm in stressful situations; nothing fazes her. And James is a fun-loving person but also very responsible and devoted to his family.

- Think about couples whose relationships you don't want to emulate. Write their names and list aspects of their relationship that seem dysfunctional or destructive or individual traits that have a negative impact on their relationship.

Example: My mom and dad. Before they were divorced, my parents fought all the time. My dad refused to talk about problems or make any changes; he was very stubborn. And my mom allowed him to treat her poorly. Up until he left her for another woman, she was tolerant of all kinds of behaviors I wouldn't want in my relationships, like cheating and staying out all night without telling her where he was.

- Based on your response to the previous question, think about what behaviors you would find intolerable in a partner, then consider what would be the opposite. In other words, what behaviors would be important to you in a partner for supporting a healthy relationship?

  Example: Instead of infidelity and staying out all night, there would be respect, trust, and fidelity. My partner will be open to talking about issues when we have a problem. Each of us will expect respect from the other, and we'll leave the relationship if that respect is repeatedly broken.

- Make a list of traits or characteristics that your ideal mate would embody or possess. After you create the list, arrange it in order of importance to you. Then, for each trait, give an example of someone you know who embodies this trait and describe how that person represents this ideal trait or value.

  Example:

  1. *Loyal. My friend Beth is a very loyal person. She's always there when I need her, she would defend me no matter what, and she never speaks poorly of others behind their backs. She's a true friend, and I would trust her with my life.*

  2. *Hardworking. I work hard in my career, and I tend to have better friendships with my friends who can relate to this value. For instance, Whitney and Taylor both understand when I'm working on deadline, whereas my friends Beth and Jeremy don't share the same attitude about work, and we've drifted apart after college, since we started working.*

- Describe the kind of partner you want to be. What would you like to offer in a relationship? What are some of the traits you possess that could be valuable to a potential partner?

  Example: I want to be a loving and caring partner. What I can offer a partner is my generous and caring nature, my affection, and my support. I'm kind, reliable, and hardworking. I take good care of myself and cook healthy meals. My friends find my kindness and reliability valuable. My family appreciates that I'm generous and caring and always look out for them. I think a future partner would appreciate what I have to offer because these are traits my friends and family value.

- Describe how you'd like to feel about yourself when you're with your ideal partner. How do you imagine interacting with this person?

  Example: I'd like to feel confident, secure, and healthy around my partner. I want to be able to be myself and be loved in spite of my flaws. I imagine I'd be able to make my partner feel good too. In my ideal world, we'd make each other laugh and have a blast together, but also be comfortable having quiet, relaxing time together.

- What kind of a physical relationship would you like to have? Do you enjoy giving and receiving affection? What kind of a sex life would you like to have?

  Example: I'm not a big fan of public displays of affection, but holding hands or having our arms around each other would be nice. Sex is important to me and I want to have a partner I'm attracted to and who's comfortable exploring and enjoying our sex life together.

It's possible that some of these questions were more difficult than others for you to answer. For instance, some of the clients I've worked with haven't been around couples who are happy and satisfied. When I ask them to describe happy couples, they struggle to come up with any examples. Their only experience has been of coldness, inequality, dishonesty, or resignation. Many of these clients wonder if happy relationships really even exist or if they're just a myth perpetuated by romantic movies and books.

Having Realistic Expectations

If you haven't seen others in healthy, fulfilling, loving relationships and haven't experienced one yourself, it's understandable that you may wonder whether they even exist. I can tell you definitively that while no relationship is perfect, there are indeed many, many people who are truly happy together. It isn't expecting too much to want a relationship that's mutually satisfying, respectful, committed, and meaningful, with enduring positive feelings between the two of you. Best of all, good relationships tend to deepen and get better with time.

However, becoming fixated on unrealistic standards won't be helpful. If you expect your relationship to go without a hitch or for your partner to never annoy you, you'll eventually be disappointed. We all have flaws. All couples disagree, and all relationships go through rough spells. While there will be tough times and aspects of your partner that you'll find frustrating, when you find a good match, that person's good qualities will make it easier to handle those imperfections.

Overall, having high standards for your relationships is a good thing. It's reasonable to expect that a healthy relationship will feel good much of the time. In my experience, people who are in satisfying relationships tend to report that their partner far exceeds their expectations in many ways. Imagine how nice it would feel to know that your partner truly offers what you want, and more.

You may also underestimate what you have to offer in a relationship. This is why the relationship inventory exercise encourages you to think about what you have to offer and what kind of partner you want to be. Knowing and valuing what you have to offer someone else will strongly contribute to dating success.

There are two main pieces of the equation in finding a relationship that's fulfilling for you. The first is taking a long, deep look at the values that really resonate with you. By completing the exercises in this chapter—especially the relationship inventory—and taking time to contemplate your answers, you've taken this crucial first step.

The second is allowing yourself to have hope for a fulfilling relationship. So often, people sacrifice hope because they fear being let down. It's common to think, *If I hope to meet someone I truly connect with, won't I just be disappointed if that doesn't happen?* The truth is, we can't avoid disappointment or being hurt; it's part of life. It's important to recognize that the sweet spots in life, the truly meaningful moments, may include some disappointment as well as hope.

Allowing yourself to face the possibility of disappointment and even embrace the idea of being uncomfortable is a freeing way to live. It stretches your limits and increases your capacity to experience joy and meaning in life. If you allow both hope and disappointment, both fear and excitement, to exist within you, you can embrace the good that comes your way while knowing that you can deal with whatever difficulties arise.

Only by identifying the qualities you want in a relationship can you hope to find those qualities in a partner. Doing so will also give you strength to face the disappointments that may arise along the way. With this perspective, you can interact with and respond to potential partners in a positive way, taking heart in knowing that your values and unique traits make you the kind of person a fitting partner would want to be with.

Summary

Overall, living a valued life will help you feel more comfortable in who you are and what you stand for. This will bolster you and leave you less susceptible to feeling judged by others and less influenced by fear. You'll feel more in touch with the meaning and direction in your life and therefore more satisfied with your life. Values are the foundation that you build your world on. They help you set goals and find vitality and energy. When you live in greater alignment with your values, you'll exude a sense of stability that others will sense. And just as you're probably attracted to people who know what they want in life, others will find it attractive that you have a sense of your purpose in the world.

Now that you've identified the values you hold dear and evaluated your partner preferences, you can put those values and preferences into action. Chapter 6 is devoted to helping you create a clear plan of action to bring your values to fruition. Your plan will help you create the life and dating environment you want by letting go of the idea that anxiety is holding you back and instead actively making decisions based on your values, your goals, and the future you wish to create.

CHAPTER 6

———→ ♥ ←———

Your Plan of Action

My client Chrissie was sitting in my office smiling. She told me about her date the previous night: "I almost didn't go. About an hour before I was supposed to meet Paul, I was so nervous getting ready. I was getting self-conscious and sort of shutting down. I just didn't think I could do it. I started coming up with excuses for canceling, like 'I'm not feeling well' or 'I have a friend who just went through a breakup and really needs me.' But then I stopped and thought about what we've been talking about in session. I don't want to be the kind of person who makes up excuses in order to avoid going out. I made a plan, and I wanted to stick with it. Plus, I knew if I canceled, I'd regret it and feel lonely, because I did want to get to know Paul better. The old me would have stayed home. I probably would never have agreed to go out with Paul."

She went on to say, "Change is about doing things differently, so I just reminded myself that my goals are to have fun with dating and be more flexible in how I approach things. I tried to observe my worried thoughts as they appeared but not buy into those thoughts, and then I did go out and meet Paul, even though my heart felt like it was pounding out of my chest. After the first few minutes, my anxiety got much better. We went miniature golfing, which I thought sounded weird at first, but it turned out to be pretty fun. I told Paul I wasn't very good, and he said he thought it was cute how I was embarrassed, then said not to worry because I'd be a pro by the time we left. I think I like him, so we'll see what happens. Even if it doesn't work out, I feel great that I went."

As Chrissie's story illustrates, for successful dating, the ultimate aim isn't to eliminate shyness or anxiety from your experience. In fact, trying to avoid or get rid of shyness or anxiety in the context of dating only makes you more self-conscious. That's why the goal of this book is to help you recognize this key point: it isn't necessary to be free of shy, anxious, or worried thoughts to be fulfilled and live a rich, satisfying life. Being able to tolerate upsetting thoughts or feelings and still move forward with living a valued life is what will ultimately lead to life satisfaction (Hayes and Lillis 2014). This ability to move forward—with your shyness and anxiety—will ultimately set you on the path you want to be on. When you follow your deepest values despite anxiety, worry, or self-doubt, a whole new world opens up to you—a world full of meaning and possibilities.

This chapter will help you embrace the vision for your life that you identified by exploring your values in chapter 5. Earlier chapters gave you skills to help you tolerate upsetting thoughts and feelings and still move forward when they threaten to immobilize you. Now you're ready to take committed action toward integrating your values into your life. This chapter will help you do just that.

Commitment to Action

You ultimately know what's best for you, so in this chapter I'm going to put the power in your hands. While I'll make some suggestions and guide you through the process of creating an action plan, you'll choose what to do, when to do it, and how to respond to challenges along the way. No one likes feeling like they're being forced into living a certain way, dating, or attending certain events. And no one can make you ready to change except you. This is where choice comes in.

Committed action is about choosing to be in control of living your life in a way that's meaningful, even when that requires embracing uncertainty. It's choosing to be active, not passive or avoidant, in your life. The goals you set for yourself shouldn't be tasks that you dread but feel you must accomplish because a dating book advised you to do so. Instead, the goals you set for yourself should reflect how *you* want to live. In doing so, you'll experience both ups and downs, and along the way, you'll share meaningful experiences with potential romantic interests and dates, experience moments of laughter or levity, and have the opportunity to truly connect with others. That's what makes these goals worthwhile. The aim isn't just finding a partner; it's creating a life that you want to live, with a partner you want to share it with.

One of the biggest reasons people don't make changes is because they aren't sure how to start the process. Living the life you want to live may sound exciting but also intimidating. Indecision can become a roadblock, stopping you dead in your tracks. You may not feel ready, may not be sure when you'll be ready, or wonder how you'll find the confidence to change. The simple truth is that you have to start with new behaviors, in the form of small and simple steps. Feelings of confidence will follow. Here are some ideas for how you can bolster your ability to take those steps.

Feelings Follow Actions

If we all waited until our emotions were in the "right" place to do things, say finish a work project or do the laundry, our lives wouldn't function too well. Instead of waiting for your emotions regarding dating to feel right, trust that your feelings will follow your actions. So instead of waiting until you feel comfortable to talk to a new coworker, go ahead and talk to her at her desk for a few minutes regardless of how you feel. Feelings of confidence will follow that action. Or rather than waiting until you feel like it's the right time to join a dating service, go ahead and join it despite your doubts. You'll feel ready after you've signed up, because nothing says ready more than being there. When doubt creeps in as you try to take new actions that reflect your values, remind yourself that your feelings will follow your actions.

Willingness Is Key

The main ingredient you need in order to be successful in dating and in love is willingness to have new experiences. You must be willing to engage with life and with others—to feel vulnerable, anxious, embarrassed, thrilled, and excited—and to let all of this occur while still knowing that forging a relationship may take a while. That may sound like a tall order, but if you can maintain willingness, you'll get where you want to be.

Give Yourself Permission

What's your first association with the idea of being "available"? Our society tends to see availability as a liability—as being pathetic or being desperate to find someone. This simply isn't true. Being available is an essential ingredient in establishing a new relationship.

It's okay and natural to want love and to want to give love. People may try to make you think it's abnormal or that you shouldn't want it so much. They may advise you to just be happy being single. But the truth is, it's fulfilling and wonderful to be in love. And it's okay to go looking for what you want. Being available simply means that you're open to falling in love.

Popular culture and media tend to paint an image of unavailability being cool or ideal. We can get the idea that men are supposed to play the field and try to sleep with as many women as possible, with the background thought that committing to a woman would be a drag. Women are supposed to busy themselves with friends, work, hobbies, and being fabulous, pretending that they don't want a boyfriend or that they're happy being single. But what if you aren't happy being single or playing the field? There's no reason you should have to pretend, to · yourself or to others, that finding a partner isn't meaningful to you.

That said, being available doesn't mean dropping everything in your life so you can go on dates, or entirely losing yourself in a new love interest. Continuing to work on your own emotional well-being and to participate in activities you enjoy while you're single is essential to being in a good place when you meet someone you're interested in.

The process of dating and finding a partner can take time, effort, and energy. Being honest with yourself about being available will kick-start the process and help you be authentic. Just as you might commit to going back to school or trying to advance your career, it's important to commit to spending time and energy dating and meeting people.

Sure, the stars might align and allow you to meet the right person at the right time without any effort. For some people, it happens just that way. But more often, people need to be willing to step outside their comfort zones, put themselves in places and situations where they can meet like-minded people, and take some action steps toward achieving their relationship goals.

Your Action Plan

Up to this point in the book, much of the discussion has been hypothetical. We've talked about how to handle potential dating scenarios, how to be mindful and engaged with your date, and how to defuse from potential shy and worried thoughts in dating situations. But the most important element of learning anything is to begin to practice the skills involved. And remember, the last part of that phrase that sums up the ACT approach is "Take action." This is where goal setting comes in.

Goal setting allows you to practice the techniques you've learned throughout this book by taking action. The more you practice putting your skills into action, the more comfortable you'll become with these new ways of thinking and being with others. Your tendency to be shy or anxious may mean you do well with hypothetical scenarios but find it harder to take action. Starting to test your new skills is the best way to truly make changes. Initially, the changes can be small or easy, but it's important to take that first step.

Start with a Goal and Follow Up with Specific Steps

Researchers have studied which approaches tend to work best in terms of achieving goals. Starting out with more flexible goals can be helpful in fostering willingness. But ultimately, creating a specific plan of action helps people achieve their goals (Jin et al. 2013). So in this chapter, you'll eventually create a concrete plan. If this approach starts to feel difficult, remember that creating a specific step-by-step plan is more likely to help you follow through and get what you want.

Research also shows that writing down your goals, rather than just thinking about them, makes it more likely that you'll accomplish them (Hale 2011). For this reason, it's important to actually complete the exercises in this chapter, rather than just reading through them. Additionally, telling a friend about a goal and then checking in regularly with that friend also increases the chances that you'll meet your goal (Hale 2011). Therefore, in this chapter I'll help you identify people you can share your goals with to enlist their support.

The goals you choose to set can be in any form you like, so long as it helps you implement a value you hold. For instance, here are some possible goals related to values:

➟ *I value living a full life that includes a variety of people because that helps me feel less isolated and is also more fun. In order to have more people in my life, I'm setting a goal of meeting new people.*

➟ *I value being able to attend and enjoy social events, even if that causes some discomfort. To implement this value, I'm setting a goal to attend social events more often.*

→ *I value balance in my life because this lessens my anxiety and keeps me interested and engaged. To help this value flourish, I'm setting the goal of working less on weekends and using my vacation time for relaxing or exciting trips.*

→ *I value learning and career development. To further this pursuit, I'm setting a goal of looking into MBA programs. Another goal is to do more reading on my own.*

You'll notice that some of these goals are clearly related to dating and others aren't. Some of your values may not directly relate to dating, but it's still helpful to pursue your goals in those areas because doing so will help you feel good about yourself and where you're going in life. Again, feeling self-confident can only help you in dating, and it will also increase your well-being both when you're single and when you develop a relationship.

Creating an action plan involves a few steps. The first is to identify a specific goal you want to work toward. Be realistic and choose something you actually have control over and can make happen.

Next, identify which steps will be most effective in achieving your goal. Breaking a large goal down into smaller steps will make your goal feel accessible rather than overwhelming.

Lastly, you make a commitment to follow through. If you want to work on several goals, this step will entail deciding on a realistic timeline for each. Some goals will be compatible. For instance, if your goals include spending more time with friends, engaging in more physical activity, and increasing your participation in activities where you might meet potential dates, setting a goal of participating in a coed tennis tournament or taking a yoga class with a friend might meet all of those goals. Alternatively, you may find that you don't have time to work on several goals at once, or that you need to work on different goals separately. In that case, you'll need to prioritize your goals.

Ideas for Meeting Potential Dates

One of the most common and helpful goals for shy daters is meeting or connecting with potential dates. Yet if you're like most people, you may draw a blank when brainstorming ideas about how to make this happen. Because so many clients ask me for guidance on where and how they can meet people, I've included a list of activities that can increase your chances of meeting potential partners. In addition, many of them may help you reach other goals, in areas of your life beyond dating and relationships:

→ Take up a sport or recreational activity, such as skiing, tennis, golf, volleyball, swimming, basketball, soccer, yoga, kayaking, hiking, cycling, running, and so on.

→ Ask a friend to set you up with someone who might be a good match for you.

→ Join an online dating site or download and use a dating app.

→ Take a class related to a hobby, such as chess, writing, painting or drawing, music, gardening, cooking, or photography.

→ Get involved in a specialty group. From book clubs and alumni groups to science fiction conventions and local theater groups, the possibilities are endless.

→ Sign up for a matchmaking service, speed dating, or a program like It's Just Lunch.

→ Take a continuing education course at a local college, whether related to your job or something else you're interested in. Creative writing, business, computing and IT, engineering, health, communications, media, construction, design, real estate, medicine, social sciences, law, and science are just a few of the possibilities.

→ Join a group for singles: single parents, child-free singles, singles meet-ups, social clubs, singles cruises—the list goes on. If you search online, you can find singles groups dedicated to many particular interests, from adventure to zoos.

→ Volunteer with local community organizations that fit with your interests, from helping kids or senior citizens to park cleanups or walking for a cause to working for Habitat for Humanity. Also consider organizations related to your career.

→ Accept invitations to happy hour or lunch with coworkers, or invite your coworkers out.

→ Accept invitations to and attend parties, whether at the office, with friends, or with neighbors.

→ Attend religious services or events.

→ Attend fund-raising, charity, or networking events.

→ Use social media to connect and facilitate face-to-face interactions.

→ Visit public places that have a social component: dog parks, coffee shops, bookstores, gyms, grocery stores, libraries, and so on.

→ Exercise: Setting Goals and Creating an Action Plan

Refer back to your values inventory from chapter 5 for ideas about goals you'd like to set based on the values you'd like to strengthen. As a reminder, the life domains covered in chapter 5 were intimate relationships, friendship, family, work and education, parenting, recreation, spirituality, and health and wellness. You also identified values unique to you that don't fall into these domains. For this exercise, choose three to five domains that you'd like to set goals for, keeping in mind that values-consistent actions in any area of life can enhance your well-being and the quality of your relationships with others.

Once you've set a goal in each domain, list the specific, concrete steps you need to take to reach each. The Goal and Action Plan worksheet includes space for six steps, but feel free to list fewer, or to use a separate piece of paper if you'd like to list more. An example worksheet is provided, followed by a blank one for your use. (For a downloadable version of that worksheet, visit http://www.newharbinger.com/30031, or see the back of this book for more details.)

Finn's Goal and Action Plan Worksheet

Life domains: *Intimate relationships*

Values: *My values in this domain include finding a partner I can develop a long-term relationship with who has interests similar to mine. The women I've met through work haven't really been on the same page as me, so maybe it's time to explore other avenues.*

Goal: *Meeting and connecting with potential dates with similar relationship goals*

Action step 1: *Research online dating sites and dating apps on the Web.*

Action step 2: *Ask friends for suggestions of dating sites or apps they've used and would recommend.*

Action step 3: *Choose one dating site or app and sign up.*

Action step 4: *Complete my profile.*

Action step 5: *Browse profiles for twenty minutes.*

Action step 6: *Initiate contact with three potential dates by sending a message or contact request.*

Who will you ask to help support you in this goal? *My friend Beth*

How will you ask your friend to support you in this goal? Be specific. *I'll ask her to help me create my dating profile, and I'll call her each week to update her about potential dates.*

What are potential barriers to this goal?

> **Thoughts:** *No one will like me or want to respond to me.*

> **Feelings:** *Anxious, discouraged*

What coping skills can you use when you encounter these obstacles?

> **Thoughts:** *Practice defusing from my thoughts. Remind myself that I can have a thought without buying into it. In other words, I can have those doubts and still go reach out to people.*

> **Feelings:** *Practice mindfulness and tuning in to my feelings. Rather than run from the anxiety, I'll embrace it and get used the idea that it's okay to feel discomfort. I'll also remind myself that the feelings won't last forever.*

Goal and Action Plan Worksheet

Life domains:

Values:

Goal:

Action step 1:

Action step 2:

Action step 3:

Action step 4:

Action step 5:

Action step 6:

Who will you ask to help support you in this goal?

How will you ask your friend to support you in this goal? Be specific.

What are potential barriers to this goal?

    Thoughts:

    Feelings:

What coping skills can you use when you encounter these obstacles?

    Thoughts:

    Feelings:

Your goals can be whatever you want them to be. A goal might be to complete one social mishaps exposure practice from chapter 4 each week. It might be to ask a friend to join the social club Grouper and plan group outings so you can meet new potential dates. Your goal might be to volunteer once a week for group beach cleanup and talk to someone who seems interesting while there, or it could be to attend social mixers hosted by your alumni group and introduce yourself to one new person each time. You'll know you've chosen goals that align with your values when you find yourself getting excited by the prospect of engaging in these activities and have a sense that doing them makes you a more active participant in creating the life you want.

To remind yourself of your goals, print them out and post them somewhere you'll see them often, to serve as a visual reminder.

──→ Exercise: Coming Up with a Worst-Case Scenario Coping Plan

On the way to reaching your goals, whether to increase the number of people you date, initiate contact with new people, accept date requests, or go out on a first date with someone, you may still hear that nagging, fearful voice that says, *This could be a complete and utter disaster!* And it's true that there's always a chance things will go poorly. Therefore, it's helpful to come up with a coping plan. This will give you more confidence in facing your fears. And on the off chance that the worst does happen, you'll be in a better position to deal with it.

So let's assume that your worst-case scenario has come to fruition—your nightmare is a reality. Perhaps you meet someone for a first date and he laughs at you when you walk up and turns to leave without saying a word. Perhaps your date doesn't show up. Perhaps your date does show up and starts to make you uncomfortable by being overly sexual. Maybe you hint to a friend that you've always liked him, and he responds that he just doesn't like you "that way" and stops talking to you. Maybe you're divorced and go out on your first date in fifteen years, and at some point the person says to you, "Wow, that's not how things are done nowadays. When's the last time you went on a date, 1998?" Maybe you ask a coworker out and she tells you she wouldn't go out with you if you were the last man on earth and that she's way out of your league. Maybe you go to sit next to a cute guy in your college English 101 class and he asks you to move, saying, "I'm saving this seat for the hot brunette."

Whatever your worst-case scenario may be, take a moment to imagine it in detail. Picture what could go wrong and how it would play out. Then focus on how you could cope if your feared scenario were to happen. Consider the following questions and write your responses in your journal:

- How could you respond in the moment? What behavioral coping skills might you use? Examples include assessing the situation from an objective observer perspective, doing some mindful breathing, or practicing assertiveness by removing yourself politely but firmly from the situation. You might come up with a few basic go-to sentences you could use to help you leave if you needed to.

- Afterward, how could you cope emotionally? What skills would you use? Examples include tuning in to your emotions with acceptance, labeling them, and extending compassion to yourself and your feelings. You might also engage in self-care activities, like calling friends and asking them to spend time with you, attending a sports event, going out to dinner, going shopping, or relaxing by taking a hot bath or shower or reading a good book.

- How could you cope with your thoughts? What skills would you use? Examples including watching the thought snowball, becoming a distant observer, thanking your mind, and labeling thoughts.

- Who could you turn to for support? Name specific friends or family who would be there for you.

My client Dennis was worried that he'd run out of topics for conversation on a date, and that his date would then be bored or laugh at him behind his back afterward. For his coping plan, he decided to come up with some stock conversation starters he could use if there was a lull in the conversation, like "Tell me about where you grew up" and "Tell me about your work," as well as follow-up questions, like "What did you like about it?" or "Why didn't you like it?" He planned to cope emotionally by reflecting on the date with compassionate attention, lifting the burden of his expectations for himself by remembering that both parties have to contribute for a date to be successful, and that the responsibility isn't his alone. He decided he'd cope with any negative thoughts by labeling his thoughts, rating their intensity, practicing willingness to feel the emotions triggered by his thoughts, and accepting those emotions, while also reminding himself that he can have thoughts without buying into them. In terms of self-care, he found that waxing his car or polishing his shoes tended to help him regain composure and focus.

As for worrying that his date would laugh about him behind his back, he decided he'd remind himself that he can't control what other people might do or say. Lastly, he identified people he could call: his sister and his friend Mike, who would both be supportive. He also thought it would be a good idea to plan to get together with friends after dates; that way he'd have a built-in support plan and would also place less emphasis on a date because he had other plans afterward.

Now that you've considered Dennis's example and envisioned an effective coping plan for yourself, have your feelings about your worst-case scenario changed? Hopefully you feel less fearful and less overwhelmed by the thought of that situation because you now know it's manageable. Maybe you even feel empowered and motivated to take risks, knowing that you have a way to cope with difficulties that might arise.

Making Meaning Out of Hardships

Most of us have a tendency to view hardships as setbacks and failures that prevent us from achieving our goals. But what if you could see hardships as an important, even necessary part of living a full life? It's impossible to be happy, successful, and carefree all the time. Part of the package in life is accepting that hard times will occur, and that they can be an avenue for growth, and therefore part of what makes you an intriguing person.

To see how this works, think about someone you want to date or someone you've liked in the past. What do you admire about that person? What hardships has that person endured? Did that person always perform flawlessly in every situation? The answer to that last question is probably no. The people we admire and want to be with tend to be those who have persevered and overcome adversity in spite of setbacks.

Now apply those same standards to yourself. Think about the times when you've struggled the most. Did you learn anything about yourself? Did those experiences make you stronger or wiser? When you can find meaning in hardships rather than being discouraged by them, you realize that tough experiences are part of what makes you an appealing, complex individual.

Instead of being averse to failure or rejection, try giving yourself permission to set challenging goals and sometimes fail or be rejected. Along the way, you'll learn lessons that will help you make space for growth and insight. Here, the goal is less about achieving a desired outcome and more about learning to expand your comfort zone. This will help you become stronger, more confident, and more self-assured. You might create a mantra for yourself about this, such as "My mission is to see this goal through, work my hardest, and be kind to myself throughout the process."

Facing the Worst, Embracing the Best

Hopefully this chapter has given you some strategies that make reaching your goals seem more realistic. Even so, sometimes you may feel that life is full of hard work, pain, or rejection, leading to a sense of hopelessness. It can be daunting to contemplate embracing your shyness, anxiety, or fear. However, the flip side is that you also get to embrace all of the good moments.

Recall the sweet spot exercise in chapter 5, in which you heightened one simple, pleasurable moment from your past. You can look for these kinds of moments each and every day. Seeing the beauty in your daily life is a wonderful defense against hopelessness.

As mentioned, research has shown that shy and anxious people have more trouble savoring positive experiences, tending to respond to them by downplaying positive emotions. Whereas a nonanxious person might have a good experience and try to heighten it by reflecting on the experience, people who are anxious tend to do things to shut down these positive feelings—things as simple as saying to themselves, *This good feeling is sure to end soon* (Eisner, Johnson, and Carver 2009). This can have a variety of causes: you might be preoccupied with anxious or shy thoughts that block out the positives; you don't want to set yourself up for disappointment so you avoid feeling hopeful or trying to get what you want; you may be uncomfortable with intense emotions, including intense positive emotions; or you might be fearful of showing any signs of strong emotion in social settings, including positive emotions, for fear of embarrassing yourself or conveying too much emotion (Eisner, Johnson, and Carver 2009).

However, when you're less able to focus on and relish happy feelings, you miss out on personal enjoyment. You also miss out on sharing happy experiences with others, including dates. It makes it harder to focus on the lighthearted, fun aspects of dating and getting to know others. It also makes it harder to show how you feel about someone when you like that person and enjoy spending with them.

The solution is to actively focus on heightening your good experiences, reveling in them and being more connected with them. When you're focused on savoring positive moments, the hardships you may experience won't seem as overwhelming or devastating. You'll have the balanced perspective that comes from knowing that there's good in the world and experiencing more positive emotions.

⟶ **Exercise:** Savoring Positive Experiences

If savoring and heightening positive experiences and emotions doesn't come naturally for you, that's okay. It's a skill you can work to improve, using your five senses to notice these happy moments, and then using mindfulness to savor them. When pleasant moments arise, tell yourself, *This is a good feeling, and I want to enjoy things just as they are right now.* Be stubborn and relentless about noticing the good in life. Here are some specific recommendations for positive experiences you can savor using your five senses:

- **Sight:** artwork, the colors of a sunset, beautifully made clothing, exquisite cars, fine architecture, the curve of a path, a pretty drive, a beautiful animal or bird, pictures of people you love, scenes from vacations that you remember fondly, or beautiful landscapes, from mountains and forests to a quiet lake or the vastness of the ocean

- **Touch:** a hot bath, a cozy blanket, a warm sweater, petting a dog or cat, getting a hug, cuddling your date, holding a niece's or nephew's hand, getting a massage, feeling the cool water as you swim laps, or picking fresh blackberries or strawberries

- **Sound:** your favorite music, birds chirping, a stream gurgling, the voice of a good friend on the phone, the crackling of a fire, or the sounds of cooking a nice meal

- **Taste:** eating delicious food, drinking a cup of tea or fresh coffee, savoring a dessert, or slowly eating a piece of fruit and savoring each and every bite

- **Smell:** the aroma of your favorite foods as they cook, flowers, scented candles, scents that remind you of fond memories, fresh air after a rain, appealing perfume or cologne, or the aroma of hot coffee as you bring it to your lips

You can also set an intention to notice opportunities to savor positive emotions and thoughts:

- **Emotions:** Seek to notice and revel in peaceful, contented, or happy emotions whenever they arise, such as feeling loved, feeling appreciated, giving praise, feeling safe, feeling free, being independent, sharing laughter, being silly, feeling inspired, helping someone out, showing affection, being supportive, and so on.

- **Thoughts:** Allow yourself to linger on happy thoughts when they arise. For example: *I love being around Sasha*; *I'm hopeful right now*; *That book was touching*; *I'm inspired by this*; *Life is good*; *I've accomplished a lot today*; *I'm a nice person*; *This place is wonderful*; *I love my home*; *I have a really good family*; *Life is good*; *I'm lucky to be here*; *That movie really moved me*; or *I'm happy in this moment*.

Cultivating an approach of allowing yourself to feel and enjoy good moments will help you create more of those moments. In addition, increasing positive emotions is associated with higher self-esteem and well-being (Eisner, Johnson, and Carver 2009). And as you begin to savor positive experiences more often and intentionally, you may start surrounding yourself with people who make you laugh, become more open to different settings where you're likely to find enjoyment, and start savoring quiet moments in a way that fills you with hope and gratitude. You'll begin to bring positivity and joy to others by being encouraging, optimistic, and giving towards them. You'll also build feelings of hope and gratitude for all aspects of your life, including dating and your relationships with others (Emmons and McCullough 2003). These qualities will be apparent to those around you, and they're likely to find it appealing.

Summary

This chapter has been about moving away from hypothetical dating scenarios and toward actual changes in your life and approach to dating. To this end, you created a clear plan of action that will help you live in greater alignment with your values. You've bolstered your confidence by creating a plan for coping with your worst-case scenarios, and you've also learned about finding meaning in hardships and savoring good moments mindfully. All of these strategies will increase your ability to start creating the kind of life you desire. Then, as you approach each day with a sense of adventure and purpose, you'll also increase your chances of meeting people, including someone with whom you might build a loving, long-term relationship.

In the next chapter, we'll take a look at skills that can help you navigate the territory ahead: dating and forging new relationships. From breaking up to making a new relationship stronger, the final chapter will help you move forward confidently as you take relationships to the next level of emotional and physical intimacy.

CHAPTER 7

—➤ ♥ ◄—

Skills for Dating and Nurturing Your New Relationship

The early stages of dating are exhilarating, but are often also filled with new questions at every turn: How often will you see each other? How will you handle meeting the other person's family or introducing a potential love interest to yours? When will you discuss being exclusive? What do you do after your first fight? How and when do you share your vulnerabilities? How do you handle any anxiety or shyness that may arise due to increasing sexual intimacy? How can you develop a good physical relationship? How can you end the relationship if it isn't working? How do you communicate when you're upset? How do you ensure you're being a good partner? All of these questions can be overwhelming, especially if you tend to avoid conflict and withdraw from intense emotions.

This chapter will help you navigate this challenging territory. It offers strategies for a wide variety of relationship issues:

➤ Becoming exclusive and developing emotional intimacy

➤ Handling rejection or unreciprocated feelings

➤ Breaking up with someone

→ Developing sexual intimacy

→ Building relationship skills for addressing conflict and engaging with each other in a positive way

Becoming Exclusive

Being uncertain about whether the other person feels the same way about you is a hallmark of the early stages of a relationship. But if the relationship endures, it will eventually be important to address that uncertainty. You'll want to share with each other that you do indeed care for one another and figure out how to discuss commitment or taking your relationship to the next level. You may wonder what should be happening in your relationship for that discussion to be appropriate. Choosing to commit to someone usually involves increasing emotional intimacy and vulnerability, as well as increasing physical intimacy and affection. I'll address emotional intimacy now and sexual intimacy later in the chapter.

Increasing emotional intimacy means making yourself vulnerable in the presence of this person, sharing your inner feelings, thoughts, needs, and desires. Being intimate in this way is how people establish a real connection. It happens when the person you're dating shares something with you, such as dreams for the future, and you in turn reciprocate, sharing your dreams for the future. Or perhaps your date shares a story of loss or defeat—a time when things were really hard. In return, you become more comfortable sharing parts of yourself that feel more vulnerable. Seeking out your partner for support, comfort, and a sense of security is what strong relationships are built on (Mikulincer and Shaver 2007).

People who are shy and socially anxious, however, often have a harder time reciprocating increased intimacy. This means you may not respond to your partner's disclosure of intimate information with your own self-disclosure (Meleshko and Alden 1993). Similarly, you may feel less comfortable showing warmth or giving affection because you fear the other person will disapprove of you or judge you. Unfortunately, the end result of these attempts to protect yourself may be that your date feels and behaves less warmly toward you. In other words, if you're less open and try to protect yourself, your date may feel less connected to you and close up. So rather than avoiding the other person's disapproval, you may actually end up eliciting it (Rodebaugh et al. 2010).

This is a vicious cycle because it prevents you from building the kind of strong relationship that can help you know and believe such relationships exist, which can lead you to be even more self-protective and distrustful. Fortunately, you can break this cycle of negative interactions. As you work toward taking a relationship to the next level, you can choose to allow yourself to be vulnerable. You can choose to take a risk and disclose more about yourself and how you feel about the other person.

Allowing Yourself to Need Someone

Developing and maintaining intimacy in a close relationship requires engaging with your partner in ways that create *interdependence*. Interdependence develops when two people regularly share their intimate thoughts and feelings, express affection to each other, ask for and give support to each other, and forgive one another. Research shows that engaging in this way increases the closeness, intimacy, and satisfaction that people feel in their relationships (Collins and Miller 1994). Interdependence develops gradually, over time, and is a key component in long-term, committed relationships.

Creating interdependence in a new relationship requires that you let the other person know how you feel. Let her know that you think about her when she's not around. Tell him you thought of him when you were on a work trip and brought him a souvenir. If you've had a fight with a friend and feel upset, get together with your partner and let her soothe you; give her the power to make you feel better with a hug and kind words of comfort. When you see that your partner is struggling or needs you, be there for him emotionally. Tell your partner how much you care about her, how she makes you happy, and how you're starting to fall for her.

Taking a Risk

In some ways, risk is inherent in sharing, being vulnerable, and needing someone. There's always a chance that your new partner could reject you or respond in a way that lets you down. You may worry, *What if he doesn't show affection in return? What if she ignores me when I ask for support? What if he thinks I'm silly or needy for bringing him a souvenir? What if she doesn't feel the same way about me?* These responses from someone you like and care for can understandably cause you to feel hurt or dissatisfied, presenting a dilemma: on one hand, you want to form a close, interdependent relationship, but on the other, you also want very much not to be rejected or hurt. To find your path forward, ask yourself a key question: *Is this someone I believe I can safely risk being vulnerable with?* If the answer is yes, then ask yourself, *What would I be missing by holding back?*

While there's no way to guarantee that you won't get hurt, you can usually trust your instincts when you start to develop feelings for someone who clearly reciprocates. And while you do have to take a risk to see if the other person could be a good partner for you, keep in mind that the other person is also looking for someone who can be supportive, affectionate, and open. Most people want to find someone who can give them the safe feeling that comes with interdependence and a close bond. People want to feel cared for and loved.

To increase sharing, communication, and intimacy, try disclosing some of the following types of information to the person you're interested in:

→ Share stories from your past that let him know more about you and who you are today. Ask about his past and favorite memories.

→ Share how she makes you feel. Does she make you feel light-hearted? Does she make little things fun? Is cooking a meal with her more fun than cooking on your own? Let her know.

→ Express what you like about him, such as how he's passionate about learning new things, how fearless he is when it comes to traveling, or how he shares your love of reading.

→ Let her know what you appreciate about her personality or the way she conducts herself. What special qualities make her stand out from others?

→ Share your hopes or aspirations for the future with him. Let him know what motivates you toward those goals and what they mean to you.

→ Disclose your willingness to try new things with her or join him in his favorite hobby.

→ Share about experiences you'd like to have with her in the future. Do you want her to meet your Aunt Ilsa because you know she'd love her? Do you think you two would have a blast exploring the streets of your hometown together? Share it!

→ Do you want to be exclusive and not see anyone else because you like him so much? Let him know you're not interested in seeing anyone else.

There's no perfect way to time these disclosures. Every relationship proceeds at its own pace depending on the people involved. But you can take the lead in increasing intimacy by disclosing a bit of personal information and seeing how the other person responds. As you build trust with one another, you can begin sharing more significant information and allowing yourself to be more vulnerable. In this way, you can strengthen the relationship.

———➤ **Exercise:** Using Mindfulness to Promote Connection with Your Partner

Some clients tell me that even though they like their partner, it's difficult for them to connect to strong feelings or feel particularly close to others. Research has shown that mindfulness meditation can help prime the brain for bonding (Atkinson 2013). This approach involves focusing your attention on an intention for your intimacy-related feelings to increase.

More specifically, spend five minutes each day mindfully contemplating things that help promote intimate, close feelings toward your partner. For instance, you can start out by considering where your partner is and what she's doing as you engage in this meditation. When you have a clear picture of what your partner is doing, think kind thoughts about her and wish her well. Alternatively you might bring to mind some happy times you've had with your partner and replay those moments. You could picture the ways your partner helps you or contributes to the relationship. You might spend some time thinking about things you can do to make your partner feel happy or ease some of the stress of his day. Or simply review the things you like about your partner and how he's made your life better. By dwelling on the positive aspects of the other person and your attachment to her, you're training your brain to become more attached, committed, and open to her.

In addition to meditating upon these things, you can take this approach a step further by acting on some of those thoughts. Send him a text just to let him know you're thinking of him, or send him a funny link that might make him smile. Stop on the way home and buy her fresh flowers or a bottle of wine she'd enjoy. If you're walking together, grab his hand and tell him you're having a good time. Use mindful awareness to help you take action and express what's on your mind.

Handling Rejection or Unreciprocated Feelings

Not all relationships work out, and sometimes the decision to end things may not be your choice. Whether rejection is subtle or overt, it's almost always difficult to handle. At the subtle end of the spectrum, Venessa went on a few dates with Jay, a guy she'd been friends with for several years. After ending a relationship with a long-term girlfriend, Jay started pursuing Venessa, but to Venessa, it seemed as though things never really progressed. Their intimacy wasn't increasing, and she didn't feel that Jay wanted to deepen the bond. Then he started contacting her less, and eventually he told her he thought they were better off as friends. This was difficult for Venessa to handle because it seemed that Jay went from being interested and engaged to being distant and withdrawing for no real reason. She still had strong feelings for him, but he'd moved on.

These kinds of unreciprocated feelings can be very painful to deal with, but there are several ways you can cope with rejection. The first is to try to minimize rejection by paying attention to the other person's cues. By observing the other person mindfully and listening to your own instincts, you may be able to pick up on rejection cues earlier than you otherwise would. Listen to your inner voice when it says things like *He seems to be quite the ladies' man; maybe he's not up for a relationship* or *She seems hung up on her last boyfriend; maybe she's not ready for a relationship yet.*

And whether the other person's cues are subtle or overt, try not to make rejection worse by pursuing someone who isn't interested or available. You might wonder why anyone, especially people who are anxious or shy, would seek out someone who seems likely to reject them in the long run. The answer is that someone who's unavailable may reject them, but that person probably won't ever get close enough to love them and form a bond, which might be what they're really afraid of. If you're afraid of intimacy, seeking out someone who's unavailable makes painful rejection likely, but it's also a way of staying emotionally safe.

Of course, it's also possible to be rejected by someone you genuinely like and hope to have a relationship with. For example, Christie found herself more drawn to Dave on each date. They saw each other for about a month, and things seemed to be going really well. But then Dave stopped calling as much, telling Christie that he'd gotten really busy. When Christie tried to contact him a few times and he didn't return her calls, she became increasingly upset. She texted him saying that she really missed seeing him and hoped that they were going to keep hanging out. After not receiving a response to her text, she decided to stop by the bar where he watched football with his friends on Sundays. He didn't react well to her arrival; after awkwardly saying hello, he essentially ignored her while she sat next to him. Then, at one point he got up and started talking to another girl. Christie felt painfully rejected.

Where did Christie go wrong? She didn't do anything obvious to cause Dave to reject her, and she may never know why Dave lost interest. But she heightened the painfulness of his rejection by continuing to pursue him after he showed clear disinterest. After the first few times someone cancels, declines an invitation, or claims to be busy, it's probably best to let it go or to leave it to the other person to make another move. You may want to avoid calling or texting the person or leaving Facebook messages. You might want to resist the urge to try to run into her in places where she hangs out or ask a mutual friend what she's up to. Pursuing someone who's disinterested will probably make you feel worse.

You may find that even though you're no longer pursing the relationship, you still miss a former love interest, especially if you developed strong feelings for the person. It's completely normal to miss an ex, even if you know the relationship wasn't working. You may need a healing period. Give yourself some time to feel your feelings and grieve the relationship. Allow yourself to feel disappointed, upset, hurt, and distraught. Journal or talk to a friend. Express your emotions. Perhaps you feel it's unfair or you've become discouraged about love. Then, after allowing yourself to experience your feelings, take some time to reflect on the relationship: What did you learn from it? How would you like your next relationship to be different? This kind of self-reflection can be helpful. But be aware that too much self-reflection can become rumination—going over the same problems or regrets over and over, which can keep you stuck rather than moving forward.

Finally, it's essential to comfort and encourage yourself. Fortify yourself with positive messages based in your values, and recommit to your goals. With self-compassion, remind yourself that this is what the journey to finding love looks like, and that one rejection doesn't mean the end of your story of falling in love. And in addition to encouraging yourself, continue to engage in activities that help you feel aligned with your core values. Commit to spending time with people you care about or engaging with new people, investing in healthy attachments.

Breaking Up with Someone

Is it difficult for you to think about ending a relationship, even if you know it's not right for you? Perhaps your anxiety tells you that you're being unkind or rude, or that it's too embarrassing to be so firm. But part of overcoming anxiety is remembering that you want to keep your values and goals in mind. If you ultimately value being able to move past your anxiety, then you can challenge yourself to be firm and clear about your feelings when doing so helps you reach your dating and relationship goals. Staying on a date where you feel miserable or continuing a relationship with someone you don't really care for will only make your anxiety worse. Call up some confidence in your ability to set boundaries when you need to, and then do it. This will empower you to branch out and date other people, and to recognize that you can end relationships that aren't right for you.

It's common to like someone a lot at first and then, after being together a few months and getting to know each other better, to recognize that the two of you aren't a good match. This is a natural process. You can't help it if someone isn't the right person for you, and just because you hit it off at first doesn't mean you have to spend the rest of your lives together.

When breaking up with someone, remember that even though it may temporarily hurt the other person, it isn't going to end his world or devastate him for too long. People are resilient. Breaking up is just part of dating and figuring out who is and isn't a good fit for you. Also bear in mind that it's the fair thing to do. You probably wouldn't want someone to keep dating you even if she wasn't very excited about you, so this gives her the same consideration.

Probably the worst and most painful way to approach breaking up is to simply ignore someone or not return calls. In addition to being irresponsible, it can feed anxiety by making you feel like you have to hide or avoid the person. Plus, this probably doesn't fit too well with your values. Even though you're shy, part of being a mature, considerate person is telling the other person when the relationship is over.

Having a direct, honest, and kind conversation is usually best. It can be over the phone or in person, depending on how many times you've seen each other or how far the relationship has progressed. It's acceptable to do it via text message or e-mail if you've only been on one date. However you deliver the message, it should be simple and clear; for example, "I've enjoyed getting to know you, but I don't think our relationship is going to progress any further. I don't think we should keep seeing each other." You don't need to give a complete explanation, especially if you've only been out on a few dates and haven't established a strong connection. At this stage, it's often a lack of chemistry or just a sense that this person is not for you.

Still, you may want to give the other person a general idea of why you're not interested, such as "We have different interests," "We're going in different directions," "I think we may not be a good fit for each other," "I'm not feeling a strong connection," "I'm not ready or looking for a serious relationship right now," "I don't feel that we'd be a good match in the long run," or "We don't seem to connect on some important issues." If you've met someone else, it's okay to explain that you've met someone you're interested in and are pursuing a relationship. When you're shy, it can be hard to be this direct, in which case it might be helpful to think about it this way: you're being direct for the other person's sake; it's a way of being respectful and treating the other person the way you'd want to be treated.

If you've seen each other more than a few times, if you've had any kind of sexual contact, or if you've been exclusive, it's probably best to talk face-to-face. You may also want to give the other person an idea of why the relationship didn't work out for you. This gives the other person an opportunity to reflect on his behavior for future relationships. Let the other person know why you don't think it's going to work as honestly as you can while sparing any painful details that might only be hurtful. You may want to give her a chance to ask questions or tell you how she feels. If you do that, it's important to stay emotionally connected to how you truly feel: if you want to break it off, remain steady in your position. Most people will be hurt but won't want to draw out the conversation.

If being this direct is hard for you due to your shyness or a tendency to avoid conflict, you might want to rehearse what you're going to say, including a line that will help you exit the conversation; for example, "I feel like I've tried to tell you honestly why I don't think this relationship is going to work, and at this point it seems like our conversation isn't helping the situation. I think it's probably best if I leave now." Being kind and respectful yet firm will help you feel dignified and assured that you've treated the other person the way you'd like to be treated.

Developing Sexual Intimacy

In dating, James tended to have a lot of trouble with the physical and sexual aspects of new relationships. Especially when he really liked a girl, he became consumed with self-doubts and self-consciousness about getting physical. These thoughts made it hard for him to enjoy being affectionate and sexually open with women. They also caused him to worry about not being able to get an erection or stay aroused, and to worry that he wasn't doing enough to satisfy his dates sexually.

Research confirms that this is a common pattern among shy and anxious people. Their thoughts tend to interfere with enjoying sexual contact, making it difficult for them to be in the moment sexually (Dove and Wiederman 2000). Obviously, this interferes with sexual intimacy and pleasure. It also interferes with developing a close relationship. And just as developing emotional intimacy with self-disclosure and emotional vulnerability is key, it's also important to develop sexual intimacy in romantic relationships. In this section, I'll help you think about intimacy and your sexuality in a mindful, accepting, and embracing way so you can overcome thoughts that may interfere with your connection.

Being physically and sexually close is a fundamental way that people connect and solidify their relationship bond. Although not everyone who is shy struggles with sexual intimacy, research has shown that shy people are more likely to struggle with cognitive distraction and performance anxiety than nonshy individuals (Karafa and Cozzarelli 1997). This often involves *spectatoring*, meaning focusing on monitoring your sexual activity and negative thoughts about yourself. This negative focus interferes with the ability to become immersed in the sensory aspects of a sexual experience (Masters and Johnson 1970).

Of course, performance anxiety, where the focus switches from sexual pleasure and arousal to worries about losing or maintaining an erection, sexual failure, or loss of arousal, also interferes with immersion in sexual interactions.

Worries or concerns stemming from cognitive distraction may include thoughts about whether your partner is satisfied with your actions and movements during sex, how your body looks or whether it's appealing to your partner, an inability to enjoy sexual activity if the lights are on, worry about the way you're touching your partner, and distraction by thoughts about your performance (Dove and Wiederman 2000). These thoughts can lead to reduced sexual arousal, lower levels of satisfaction, and a negative view of yourself as a sexual partner.

Dealing with Cognitive Distraction During Sexual Encounters

One way you can begin to form a more comfortable relationship with your sexuality is by increasing the amount of touch and affection you share with your date or partner. Touch has been shown to be an important part of relationship satisfaction and is linked to higher levels of intimacy and positive emotions (Debrot et al. 2013). Make an effort to touch your partner more often. This establishes a sensual connection throughout your time together. Try tuning in to your senses while you hold hands or cuddle or when you give or receive a massage. Notice how it feels to be close. Is there an initial spike of anxiety or wave of shyness? If so, how long does it last? Are you able to stay with the uncomfortable feelings as they pass?

Next, tune in to your experiences while you kiss and caress each other or in the early stages of foreplay. The key is to focus on sensations related to your body and your partner's body while de-emphasizing negative or critical thoughts that may arise. When you notice a negative thought, simply allow the thought to pass as you return your focus to your body and your physical experience. Here are ways you can bring your focus to your sensual experience:

→ Focus on the sensations you notice. How does the contact between you feel on your skin?

→ What do you notice about your partner's smell?

→ What type of textures do you notice—perhaps the feel of his hair, or the smoothness of her skin?

→ Focus on your body's reaction to being touched: What feels good? What types of sensations do you respond to and want more of?

→ Focus on your breathing and body. What changes do you notice in your breathing? What does it feel like to become aroused?

→ Focus on the sensations of touching your partner, noticing how she reacts when you touch her in different ways. Notice the interaction between the two of you and revel in the experience of giving and receiving touch and pleasure.

→ Notice sexual or sensual thoughts or desires that arise. Allow yourself to embrace sexual fantasies or sexual thoughts about your partner.

→ Notice your emotional reactions. There's no right way to feel. Simply notice your emotional reactions to being sensual and intimate with your partner.

Staying in the moment and bringing this type of mindful attention to sexual encounters acts as an antidote to negative self-talk. It reframes your focus from whether what you're doing is right or wrong and helps you connect to the fluid and ever-changing dynamic between the two of you. It helps you realize that connecting physically isn't about looking perfect or having the perfect move. It's about being in the moment and allowing yourself to get lost in sensual and erotic passion. Let your desire for your partner show, and accept your partner's erotic desire for you.

Give yourself permission to embrace your sexual self. Try to view your body as a sensual organ, rather than judging it based on the size of your penis or the flatness of your stomach. Learn what you like and dislike—what turns you on and what turns you off. Really spend some time exploring this. To be proficient in something, you need to devote time and energy to it. There are so many ways to explore and develop your sexuality, including masturbation, taking more time for intimacy with your partner, and exploring different types of touching, kissing, foreplay, and sexual positions.

Handling Performance Anxiety

When faced with performance anxiety, your tendency might be to focus on reaching orgasm, bringing your partner to orgasm, or maintaining your arousal. However, this focus on the end goal actually causes more anxiety, pressure, and distraction and can get in the way of desire and arousal. Instead, approach sex in a more relaxed and playful way. Focus on enjoying the sensations in the moment and the feeling of being with your partner, rather than an end goal of orgasm. (All that said, it may be a good idea to see a doctor to rule out any medical conditions that may be interfering with your arousal.)

As you develop a sexual relationship with your partner, you may find that communicating with each other about your desires, likes, and dislikes can deepen your intimacy and connection. You can convey what turns you on during sexual encounters by sighing or moaning, or more directly by saying that you like or enjoy something as it occurs. You can foster intimacy by allowing yourself to look into your partner's eyes and hold eye contact, or by being intimate with the lights on or with clothing removed. All of this builds trust and intimacy and helps you have a better sex life together.

If you tend to be inhibited, quiet, or passive during sexual encounters, you might want to try a technique known as exaggeration. It's just what it sounds like. Rather than keep your body passive during sexual activity, you immerse your whole body into the experience (Barbach 2000). You move your body more, make more sounds, breathe more deeply, and create more muscle tension. For both men and women, making sounds during sex can aid in feeling more free and uninhibited, leading to better experiences.

You can also become less shy and inhibited sexually by exploring and expanding your sexual awareness. Read books about sex and sexuality, watch erotic movies, or read erotic novels. Practice expressing your desire for your partner through touch and verbally. Your inhibitions will decrease as you become more comfortable with your sexuality, connect more mindfully with your experiences, and develop a loving and trusting relationship with your partner.

Relationship Skills

My client Timothy returned to therapy after a brief break and updated me on his relationship status: "I'm still seeing Carrie. Things are going really well. This is definitely the best relationship I've ever had. But now I'm worried about messing it up. I don't really have experience in being in a relationship." Many people feel this way in a new relationship; they want to continue on a healthy and happy path but feel unprepared or unsure how to proceed. This section outlines some effective strategies for making your relationship strong and keeping it that way.

A large body of research indicates that relationships tend to be healthiest and most satisfying when couples give each other reassurance, maintain positivity, and manage conflicts in a positive way (Dainton 2013). Giving reassurance means regularly letting your partner know that you care about him and assuring him of your love and commitment. Positivity means making an effort to have a cheerful and optimistic attitude around your partner, rather than inundating her with each and every worry, anxious thought, or frustration that you feel. Of course, being positive in general doesn't mean sweeping problems under the rug (more on this topic shortly). As for positive conflict management, this involves handling relationship problems in an open and effective way. It also means being patient with your partner, apologizing when you're wrong, and finding forgiveness for your partner when he or she errs. The key to all of these relationship skills is doing them on a regular basis so they become a natural, routine part of your relationship.

On the other hand, certain problematic behaviors can lead to dissatisfaction in relationships; these behaviors include being controlling, unfaithful, or jealous or handling conflict in ways that are destructive (Dainton 2013). Unfortunately, there are all too many ways to handle conflict destructively: avoiding your partner or avoiding topics that might cause you to argue, picking arguments, or trying to control the other person, to name a few. Because conflict resolution skills can be so important to a relationship's well-being, let's take a closer look at how to handle conflict in a helpful, positive way.

Handling Conflict

Being prepared for your first fight or argument can do wonders for a relationship. Most people don't enter a new relationship thinking, *How will I handle our fights, disappointments, and disagreements?* But in reality, the first conflict is one of the most important events in a new relationship.

People who are shy or anxious have a tendency to withdraw in response to conflict. You might think it's better to let it go. Maybe you don't want to harp on problems or seem picky or difficult. Alternatively, you just might not know how to bring up a touchy subject, so you avoid doing it. While this strategy may work in the short term, it spells trouble for long-term success.

One of the biggest problems I see in couples who come to me is a tendency to avoid talking about their problems together. Often they end up ignoring problems until the situation becomes unbearable. Then they come to me seeking help in talking about the trouble spots in their relationship. These same couples often tend to have trouble bonding. It's as though their unspoken problems detract from their ability to connect with and love each another, creating distance between them. Fortunately, when couples start discussing their problems in a constructive way, room for intimacy opens back up.

Here are some ways to address problems and relationship concerns proactively:

→ Bring up your concerns in a direct, straightforward manner that avoids blame and focuses on shared concerns and shared goals; for example, "I'd like to share with you how I've been feeling about this. I'm hoping we can work together to resolve this or make a plan we both feel good about."

→ Use mindfulness as you interact with your partner and notice any tendency to retreat, avoid, or withdraw on your part. Similarly, be aware of increasing anger or emotions that threaten to become toxic. When these emotions arise, take a distant observer perspective and notice what's happening without necessarily acting on your impulses or emotions.

→ Hear your partner out. Ask for her opinion on the topic and truly listen while suspending your own judgments. Try to understand her perspective as best you can, approaching it with openness and curiosity. Ask questions and rephrase her statements to make sure you understand: "Let me make sure I'm hearing your perspective correctly. It sounds like you're saying..."

→ Validate your partner's perspective. When you hear his stance on an issue, even if it's different from your own, let him know that you can see where he's coming from: "I can see how you might feel that way" or "I hear what you're saying, and it makes sense that you'd feel that way."

→ People tend to get upset or withdraw from a difficult topic when it makes them feel defensive. Identify what makes each of you feel defensive in the current dispute: "I have trouble talking about this because I worry that you're judging me" or "I tend to get defensive when I think I hear annoyance in your voice and feel dismissed."

→ Ask your partner to brainstorm solutions with you: "What are some ideas about what we can do differently?" or "How can we make this better?" Also be willing to give your partner a clear idea of solutions you've come up with, and ask her what she thinks of these ideas.

→ Make an inventory of what's essential for each of you in moving forward. Clarify what needs to be resolved or changed in order for both of you to truly feel good about the outcome: "Moving forward, I'd feel better if we could check in more often about how each of us is feeling" or "I need to feel respected, not criticized, when we discuss this."

Using this approach to conflict will lay the groundwork for healthy interactions for years to come. If your anxiety or shyness makes it difficult to address conflict so directly, enlist your partner's help. Let him know that you tend to avoid conflict but realize it's important to talk about problems. Encourage her to bring up problems, concerns, hurt feelings, or misunderstandings, and let her know that you're open to talking about those issues. Also let your partner know that you're making an effort to talk about things more openly and that he can help by checking in occasionally to see whether the two of you are on the same page.

When an argument or conflict occurs, it's also important to be able to make up. This includes being willing to admit when you've made a mistake or are sorry. An apology can go a long way toward healing a rift between the two of you. It's also important to be able to accept an apology, as holding on to grievances tends to breed resentment or bitter feelings. The most important part of coming together after an argument or fight is that one of you makes the first move to reconnect and that the other person accepts. This shows both of you that you can have a fight but still know that you love one another. It affirms that you can work your problems out, adding to your sense of security in the relationship.

Bringing Positivity into Your Relationship

As you can see, fostering positivity in your relationship doesn't mean ignoring problems or avoiding conflict. Rather, it's about addressing conflict in a caring and constructive way. Another key to bringing positivity into your relationship is accepting your partner for who he is and resisting the urge to criticize or try to change him. Accepting the fundamental essence of who your partner is—good and bad—is a powerful way to show your love. Yes, there are always areas that anyone can improve on, but you don't wish that your partner was someone or something she isn't. Instead, you understand that your partner isn't perfect and will have faults. You accept that your partner can't be your everything all the time. You accept that sometimes you'll be frustrated with one another and still appreciate everything your partner brings into the relationship.

Sometimes it may be hard to resist pointing out your partner's faults. Or, after a hard day, you may be tempted to take out your frustrations or worries on your partner. Resist those urges, and instead make an effort to regularly compliment your partner, talk about the positives in your life, and plan fun or exciting activities together (Kashdan et al. 2007). Shared positive experiences should be an ongoing part of your relationship, as relationships thrive on regular positive contact. Also, remember to think fondly of your partner when she isn't around. Practicing gratitude and mindfulness of intimacy-related feelings will help you tune in to and amplifying the positive, loving feelings you have for your partner (Atkinson 2013).

Lastly, and most importantly, give your partner emotional support. You can be supportive by giving hugs and other kinds of physical affection, joining him in his hobbies, writing love notes, or simply letting her know you're there for her when she's having a rough day. Showing that you care for and support your partner is the best way to ensure that your relationship continues to thrive.

Summary

Each moment, each day, each week, you have an opportunity to build the kind of relationship and the kind of life you want. Using the skills in this chapter is an ongoing journey that will continue to manifest in new ways. You'll be challenged in your relationships, especially when it comes to facing conflict or difficult topics, but you have the skills needed to address these challenges and turn them into opportunities to thrive. Self-doubt or distractions might initially be an obstacle to connecting sexually, but you have the mindful awareness to tune in to your body and your sensual side, allowing your critical thoughts to recede. You have the power to choose actions in alignment with being the kind of partner you want to be, bringing your values into your relationships as you do so. And when you hit the inevitable rough patches, you have the power to surmount relationship hurdles with strength, clarity, and dignity.

Final Thoughts

I hope that you're leaving this book with hope, love, and confidence brimming within you. My wish for you is that this book has helped create a new beginning for you as you embark on a journey toward finding the loving relationship you desire.

You've learned how attempts to avoid fear and anxiety have hurt your dating and love life, holding you back and keeping you isolated. But now you're equipped to handle your anxiety. You have options other than avoidance, and tools to use when dating anxieties and fears arise. You can approach your worries with openness by practicing self-compassion, accepting your emotions, being mindful, tuning in to and labeling your feelings, and adopting a distant observer perspective. You've ended the cycle of self-recrimination and no longer approach social situations feeling like you have to protect yourself.

You know that you are not alone in your anxiety, nor in sometimes feeling discouraged about finding love. Having doubts is something everyone experiences, and it doesn't have to stop you from pursuing your dreams. Pursuing what matters to you, what excites you, and what makes your life feel meaningful are all goals that are within your reach.

By looking at your values, both in relationships and more broadly in life, you've formed a clear vision of the kind of relationship you want, the kind of person you want to be in a relationship, and the kind of partner who would be a good fit for you. You know what you have to offer in a relationship. You're committed to being comfortable in your own skin and embracing your emotional, physical, and sexual self, and you've learned some techniques for getting there. This level of comfort in who you are releases you from the confines of shyness and anxiety. Rather than having your actions be dictated by anxiety, self-doubt, judgment, and worry, you're inspired by the larger picture: getting to live your dreams through a commitment to living in alignment with your values.

We've explored many topics throughout this book, from the roots of shyness and anxiety to getting in touch with and more comfortable with your sexuality. I've offered exercises that can help you develop mindfulness, handle painful emotions or critical thoughts, cope with social mishaps, set goals, and more. My wish is that all of this has come together to convey one essential message: You don't have to live in fear of what might go wrong. You don't have to fear being humiliated or worry about being found defective. You can move past internal barriers that have kept you lonely and isolated. You can have peace within yourself and acceptance of yourself. This inner calm and confidence in your own worth and value is the key to your happiness and to dating success.

Dating is a process of opening up, becoming vulnerable, and sharing yourself with a fitting partner. When you feel good about who you are and what you have to offer, this won't be as scary or overwhelming. In fact, you'll be able to experience the joy that relationships have to offer—something that may have been missing from your life. You now have skills that will help you connect with others. You know how to stay present even when your mind is telling you to retreat. You know how to engage with your dates in a way that makes the connection between you grow. As you respond to your dates with openness, lightheartedness, and the ability to be genuinely yourself, you'll fully experience how wonderful dating and relationships can be.

Relationships are not meant just for other people. Love isn't reserved for a certain select group. Love is for you.

References

American Psychiatric Association. 2013. *Diagnostic and Statistical Manual of Mental Disorders* (5th ed.). Arlington, VA: American Psychiatric Association.

Archuleta, K. L. 2013. "Couples, Money, and Expectations: Negotiating Financial Management Roles to Increase Relationship Satisfaction." *Marriage and Family Review* 49(5):391–411.

Atkinson, B. J. 2013. "Mindfulness Training and the Cultivation of Secure, Satisfying Couple Relationships." *Couple and Family Psychology: Research and Practice* 2(2):73–94.

Barbach, L. 2000. *For Yourself: The Fulfillment of Female Sexuality.* New York: Penguin Putnam.

Birnie, C., J. M. McClure, J. E. Lydon, and D. Holmberg. 2009. "Attachment Avoidance and Commitment Aversion: A Script for Relationship Failure." *Personal Relationships* 16(1):79–97.

Bressler, E., R. A. Martin, and S. Balshine. 2006. "Production and Appreciation of Humor as Sexually Selected Traits." *Evolution and Human Behavior* 27(2):121–130.

Chorney, D. B., and T. L. Morris. 2008. "The Changing Face of Dating Anxiety: Issues in Assessment with Special Populations." *Clinical Psychology: Science and Practice* 15(3):224–238.

Collins, N. L., and L. C. Miller. 1994. "Self-Disclosure and Liking: A Meta-Analytic Review." *Psychological Bulletin* 116(3):457–475.

Dainton, M. 2013. "Relationship Maintenance." In *Introduction to Communication Studies: Translating Scholarship into Meaningful Practice*, edited by A. Goodboy and K. Shultz. Dubuque, IA: Kendall-Hunt.

Dalrymple, K. L., and J. D. Herbert. 2007. "Acceptance and Commitment Therapy for Generalized Social Anxiety Disorder: A Pilot Study." *Behavior Modification* 31(5):543–568.

Debrot, A., D. Schoebi, M. Perrez, and A. B. Horn. 2013. "Touch as an Interpersonal Emotion Regulation Process in Couples' Daily Lives: The Mediating Role of Psychological Intimacy." *Personality and Social Psychology Bulletin* 39(10):1373–1385.

Dove, N. L., and M. W. Wiederman. 2000. "Cognitive Distraction and Women's Sexual Functioning." *Journal of Sex and Marital Therapy* 26(1):67–78.

Downey, G., A. L. Freitas, B. Michaelis, and H. Khouri. 1998. "The Self-Fulfilling Prophecy in Close Relationships: Rejection Sensitivity and Rejection by Romantic Partners." *Journal of Personality and Social Psychology* 75(2):545–560.

Eastwick, P. W., and L. A. Neff. 2012. "Do Ideal Partner Preferences Predict Divorce? A Tale of Two Metrics." *Social Psychological and Personality Science* 3(6):667–674.

Eifert, G. H., and M. Heffner. 2003. "The Effects of Acceptance Versus Control Contexts on Avoidance of Panic-Related Symptoms." *Journal of Behavior Therapy and Experimental Psychiatry* 34(3–4):293–312.

Eisner, L. R., S. L. Johnson, and C. S. Carver. 2009. "Positive Affect Regulation in Anxiety Disorders." *Journal of Anxiety Disorders* 23(5):645–649.

Emmons, R. A., and M. E. McCullough. 2003. "Counting Blessings Versus Burdens: An Experimental Investigation of Gratitude and Subjective Well-Being in Daily Life." *Journal of Personality and Social Psychology* 84(2):377–389.

Fang, A., A. T. Sawyer, A. Asnanni, and S. G. Hofmann. 2013. "Social Mishap Exposures for Social Anxiety Disorder: An Important Treatment Ingredient." *Cognitive and Behavioral Practice* 20(2):213–220.

Fisher, M. L., K. Worth, J. R. Garcia, and T. Meredith, T. 2012. "Feelings of Regret Following Uncommitted Sexual Encounters in Canadian University Students." *Culture, Health, and Sexuality* 14(1):45–57.

Fletcher, G. J. O., J. A. Simpson, G. Thomas, and L. Giles. 1999. "Ideals in Intimate Relationships." *Journal of Personality and Social Psychology* 76(1):72–89.

Garcia, J. R., S. G. Massey, A. M. Merriwether, and S. M. Seibold-Simpson. 2013. "Orgasm Experience Among Emerging Adult Men and Women: Relationship Context and Attitudes Toward Uncommitted Sex." Poster session presented at the annual convention of the Association for Psychological Science, Washington, DC.

Garcia, J. R., and C. Reiber. 2008. "Hook-Up Behavior: A Biopsychosocial Perspective." *Journal of Social, Evolutionary, and Cultural Psychology* 2(4):192–208.

Gilbert, P., and S. Procter. 2006. "Compassionate Mind Training for People with High Shame and Self-Criticism: Overview and Pilot Study of a Group Therapy Approach." *Clinical Psychology and Psychotherapy* 13(6):353–379.

Glashouwer, K. A., M. S. Vroling, P. J. de Jong, W. G. Lange, and J. de Keijser, J. 2013. "Low Implicit Self-Esteem and Dysfunctional Automatic Associations in Social Anxiety Disorder." *Journal of Behavior Therapy and Experimental Psychiatry* 44(2):262–270.

Glickman, A. R., and A. M. La Greca. 2004. "The Dating Anxiety Scale for Adolescents: Scale Development and Associations with Adolescent Functioning." *Journal of Clinical Child and Adolescent Psychology* 33(3):566–578.

Hale, E. 2011. "Goals: The Difference Between Success and Failure." *Fast Company*, December 5. http://www.fastcompany.com/1798754/goals-difference-between-success-and-failure. Accessed February 17, 2014.

Hart, T. A., D. B. Flora, S. A. Palyo, D. M. Fresco, C. Holle, and R. G. Heimberg. 2008. "Development and Examination of the Social Appearance Anxiety Scale." *Assessment* 15(1):48–59.

Hart, T. A., M. S. Jack, C. L. Turk, and R. G. Heimberg. 1999. "Issues for the Measurement of Social Phobia." In *Social Phobia: Recent Trends and Progress*, edited by H. G. M. Westenberg and J. A. den Boer. Amsterdam: Syn-Thesis Publishers.

Hayes, S. C. 2005. *Get Out of Your Mind and Into Your Life: The New Acceptance and Commitment Therapy.* Oakland, CA: New Harbinger.

Hayes, S. C., and J. Lillis. 2014. "Acceptance and Commitment Therapy Processes." In *Psychotherapy Theories and Techniques: A Reader,* edited by G. VandenBos, E. Meidenbauer, and J. Frank-McNeil. Washington, DC: American Psychological Association.

Hayes, S. C., J. B. Luoma, F. W. Bond, A. Masuda, and J. Lillis. 2006. "Acceptance and Commitment Therapy: Model, Processes, and Outcomes." *Behaviour Research and Therapy* 44(1):1–25.

Hayes, S. C., K. D. Strosahl, and K. G. Wilson. 1999. *Acceptance and Commitment Therapy: An Experiential Approach to Behavior Change.* New York: Guilford.

Heiser, N. A., S. M. Turner, and D. C. Beidel. 2003. "Shyness: Relationship to Social Phobia and Other Psychiatric Disorders." *Behaviour Research and Therapy* 41(2):209–221.

Hoffman, M. A., and H. Teglasi. 1982. "The Role of Causal Attributions in Counseling Shy Subjects." *Journal of Counseling Psychology* 29(2):132–139.

Hofmann, S. G., A. T. Sawyer, A. A. Witt, and D. Oh. 2010. "The Effect of Mindfulness-Based Therapy on Anxiety and Depression: A Meta-Analytic Review." *Journal of Consulting and Clinical Psychology* 78(2):169–183.

Hoge, E. A., E. Bui, L. Marques, C. A. Metcalf, L. K. Morris, D. J. Robinaugh, J. J. Worthington, M. H. Pollack, and N. M. Simon. 2013. "Randomized Controlled Trial of Mindfulness Meditation for Generalized Anxiety Disorder: Effects on Anxiety and Stress Reactivity." *Journal of Clinical Psychiatry* 74(8):786–792.

Jin, L., S. Huang, and Y. Zhang. 2013. "The unexpected Positive Impact of Fixed Structures on Goal Completion." *Journal of Consumer Research* 40(4):711–725.

Jinyao, Y., Z. Xiongzhao, R. P. Auerbach, C. K. Gardiner, C. Lin, W. Yuping, and Y. Shuqiao. 2012. "Insecure Attachment as a Predictor of Depressive and Anxious Symptomology." *Depression and Anxiety* 29(9):789–796.

Jobin, J., C. Wrosch, and M. F. Scheier. 2013. "Associations Between Dispositional Optimism and Diurnal Cortisol in a Community

Sample: When Stress Is Perceived as Higher Than Normal." *Health Psychology*, May 13 [epub ahead of print].

Karafa, J. A., and C. Cozzarelli. 1997. "Shyness and Reduced Sexual Arousal in Males: The Transference of Cognitive Interference." *Basic and Applied Social Psychology* 19(3):329–344.

Kashdan, T. B., and J. D. Herbert. 2001. "Social Anxiety Disorder in Childhood and Adolescence: Current Status and Future Directions." *Clinical Child and Family Psychology Review* 4(1):37–61.

Kashdan, T. B., J. R. Volkmann, W. E. Breen, and S. Han. 2007. "Social Anxiety and Romantic Relationships: The Costs and Benefits of Negative Emotion Expression Are Context-Dependent." *Journal of Anxiety Disorders* 21(4):475–492.

Kashdan, T. B., J. W. Weeks, and A. A. Savostyanova. 2011. "Whether, How, and When Social Anxiety Shapes Positive Experiences and Events: A Self-Regulatory Framework and Treatment Implications." *Clinical Psychology Review* 31(5):786–799.

Kashdan, T. B., M. J. Zvolensky, and A. C. McLeish. 2008. "Anxiety Sensitivity and Affect Regulatory Strategies: Individual and Interactive Risk Factors for Anxiety-Related Symptoms." *Journal of Anxiety Disorders* 22(3):429–440.

Kessler, R. C., P. Berglund, O. Demler, R. Jin, K. R. Merikangas, and E. E. Walters. 2005. "Lifetime Prevalence and Age-of-Onset Distributions of DSM-IV Disorders in the National Comorbidity Survey Replication." *Archives of General Psychiatry* 62(6):593–602.

Kircanski, K., M. D. Lieberman, and M. G. Craske. 2012. "Feelings into Words: Contributions of Language to Exposure Therapy." *Psychological Science* 23(10):1086–1091.

Kocovski, N. L., J. Fleming, and N. A. Rector. 2009. "Mindfulness and Acceptance-Based Group Therapy for Social Anxiety Disorder: An Open Trial." *Cognitive and Behavioral Practice* 16(3):276–289.

Leary, M. R., R. M. Kowalski, and C. Campbell. 1988. "Self-Presentational Concerns and Social Anxiety: The Role of Generalized Impression Expectancies." *Journal of Research in Personality* 22(3):308–321.

Leary, M. R., E. B. Tate, C. E. Adams, A. B. Allen, and J. Hancock. 2007. "Self-Compassion and Reactions to Unpleasant Self-Relevant Events:

The Implications of Treating Oneself Kindly." *Journal of Personality and Social Psychology* 92(5):887–904.

Leck, K. 2006. "Correlates of Minimal Dating." *Journal of Social Psychology* 146(5):549–567.

Levinson, C. A., T. L. Rodebaugh, E. K. White, A. R. Menatti, J. W. Weeks, J. M. Iacovino, and C. S. Warren. 2013. "Social Appearance Anxiety, Perfectionism, and Fear of Negative Evaluation: Distinct or Shared Risk Factors for Social Anxiety and Eating Disorders?" *Appetite* 67(August):125–133.

Lewis, M. A., H. Granato, J. A. Blayney, T. W. Lostutter, and J. R. Kilmer. 2012. "Predictors of Hooking Up Sexual Behaviors and Emotional Reactions Among U.S. College Students." *Archives of Sexual Behavior* 41(5):1219–1229.

Linehan, M. M. 1993. *Skills Training Manual for Treating Borderline Personality Disorder*. New York: Guilford.

Luoma, J., and S. C. Hayes. 2003. "Cognitive Defusion." In *Cognitive Behavior Therapy: Applying Empirically Supported Techniques in Your Practice*, edited by W. T. O'Donohue, J. E. Fisher, and S. C. Hayes. New York: Wiley.

Marlatt, G. A., and J. L. Kristeller. 1999. "Mindfulness and Meditation." In W. R. Miller (ed.), *Integrating Spirituality into Treatment*. Washington, DC: American Psychological Association.

Masters, W. H., and V. E. Johnson. 1970. *Human Sexual Inadequacy*. Boston: Little Brown.

McKnight, P. E., and T. B. Kashdan. 2009. "Purpose in Life as a System That Creates and Sustains Health and Well-Being: An Integrative, Testable Theory." *Review of General Psychology* 13(3):242–251.

McNally, R. J. 1989. "Is Anxiety Sensitivity Distinguishable from Trait Anxiety? Reply to Lilienfeld, Jacob, and Turner (1989)." *Journal of Abnormal Psychology* 98(2):193–194.

Meleshko, K. G., and L. E. Alden. 1993. "Anxiety and Self-Disclosure: Toward a Motivational Model." *Journal of Personality and Social Psychology* 64(6):1000–1009.

Mikulincer, M., and P. R. Shaver. 2007. *Attachment in Adulthood: Structure, Dynamics, and Change*. New York: Guilford.

Moscovitch, D. A. 2009. "What Is the Core Fear in Social Phobia? A New Model to Facilitate Individualized Case Conceptualization and Treatment." *Cognitive and Behavioral Practice* 16(2):123–134.

Mounts, N. S., D. P. Valentiner, K. L. Anderson, and M. K. Boswell. 2006. "Shyness, Sociability, and Parental Support for the College Transition: Relation to Adolescents' Adjustment." *Journal of Youth and Adolescence* 35(1):68–77.

Neff, K. 2003. "Self-Compassion: An Alternative Conceptualization of a Healthy Attitude Toward Oneself." *Self and Identity* 2(2):85–101.

Neff, K. D., K. Kirkpatrick, and S. S. Rude. 2007. "Self-Compassion and Adaptive Psychological Functioning." *Journal of Research in Personality* 41(1):139–154.

Nelson, L. J., L. M. Padilla-Walker, S. Badger, C. McNamara Barry, J. S. Carroll, and S. D. Madsen. 2008. "Associations Between Shyness and Internalizing Behaviors, Externalizing Behaviors, and Relationships During Emerging Adulthood." *Journal of Youth and Adolescence* 37(5):605–615.

Rapaport, M. H. 2001. "Prevalence, Recognition, and Treatment of Comorbid Depression and Anxiety." *Journal of Clinical Psychiatry* 62(24):6–10.

Reiss, S., and R. J. McNally. 1985. "Expectancy Model of Fear." In *Theoretical Issues in Behavior Therapy*, edited by S. Reiss and R. R. Bootzin. San Diego, CA: Academic Press.

Rivas-Vazquez, R. A., D. Saffa-Biller, I. Ruiz, M. A. Blais, and A. Rivas-Vazquez. 2004. "Current Issues in Anxiety and Depression: Comorbid, Mixed, and Subthreshold Disorders." *Professional Psychology: Research and Practice* 35(1):74–83.

Rodebaugh, T. L., M. O. Gianoli, E. Turkheimer, and T. F. Oltmanns. 2010. "The Interpersonal Problems of the Socially Avoidant: Self and Peer Shared Variance." *Journal of Abnormal Psychology* 119(2):331–340.

Roisman, G. I., A. S. Masten, J. D. Coatsworth, and A. Tellegen. 2004. "Salient and Emerging Developmental Tasks in the Transition to Adulthood." *Child Development* 75(1):123–133.

Romero-Canyas, R., and G. Downey. 2013. "What I See When I Think It's About Me: People Low in Rejection-Sensitivity Downplay Cues of

Rejection in Self-Relevant Interpersonal Situations." *Emotion* 13(1):104–117.

Rosellini, A. J., L. A. Rutter, M. L. Bourgeois, B. O. Emmert-Aronson, and T. A. Brown. 2013. "The Relevance of Age of Onset to the Psychopathology of Social Phobia." *Journal of Psychopathology and Behavioral Assessment* 35(3):356–365.

Rowsell, H. C., and R. J. Coplan. 2013. "Exploring Links Between Shyness, Romantic Relationship Quality, and Well-Being." *Canadian Journal of Behavioural Science* 45(4):287–295.

Sauer-Zavala, S., J. F. Boswell, M. W. Gallagher, K. H. Bentley, A. Ametaj, and D. H. Barlow. 2012. "The Role of Negative Affectivity and Negative Reactivity to Emotions in Predicting Outcomes in the Unified Protocol for the Transdiagnostic Treatment of Emotional Disorders." *Behaviour Research and Therapy* 50(9):551–557.

Schmidt, L. A., and N. A. Fox. 1995. "Individual Differences in Young Adults' Shyness and Sociability: Personality and Health Correlates." *Personality and Individual Differences* 19(4):455–462.

Schröder-Abé, M., and A. Schütz. 2011. "Walking in Each Other's Shoes: Perspective Taking Mediates Effects of Emotional Intelligence on Relationship Quality." *European Journal of Personality* 25(2):155–169.

Sieber, K. O., and L. S. Meyers. 1992. "Validation of the MMPI – 2 Social Introversion Subscales." *Psychological Assessment* 4(2):185–189.

Sparrevohn, R. M., and R. M. Rapee. 2009. "Self-Disclosure, Emotional Expression, and Intimacy Within Romantic Relationships of People with Social Phobia." *Behaviour Research and Therapy* 47(12):1074–1078.

Spielmann, S. S., G. MacDonald, J. A. Maxwell, S. Joel, D. Peragine, A. Muise, and E. Impett. 2013. "Settling for Less out of Fear of Being Single." *Journal of Personality and Social Psychology* 105(6):1049–1073.

Stein, M. B., and J. M. Gorman. 2001. "Unmasking Social Anxiety Disorder." *Journal of Psychiatry and Neuroscience* 26(3):185–189.

Teyber, E., and F. McClure. 2011. *Interpersonal Process in Therapy: An Integrative Model.* Belmont, CA: Brooks/Cole.

Thomas, S. E., C. L. Randall, and M. H. Carrigan. 2003. "Drinking to Cope in Socially Anxious Individuals: A Controlled Study." *Alcoholism: Clinical and Experimental Research* 27(12):1937–1943.

Thomas, S. E., A. K. Thevos, and C. L. Randall. 1999. "Alcoholics With and Without Social Phobia: A Comparison of Substance Use and Psychiatric Variables." *Journal of Studies on Alcohol* 60(4):472–479.

University of Hertfordshire. 2012. "Happiness: It's Not in the Jeans." *Science Daily*, March 8. http://www.sciencedaily.com/releases/2012/03/120308062537.htm.

Wenzel, A., J. Graff-Dolezal, M. Macho, and J. R. Brendle. 2005. "Communication and Social Skills in Socially Anxious and Nonanxious Individuals in the Context of Romantic Relationships." *Behaviour Research and Therapy* 43(4):505–519.

Wilson, K. G., and E. K. Sandoz. 2008. "Mindfulness, Values, and the Therapeutic Relationship in Acceptance and Commitment Therapy." In *Mindfulness and the Therapeutic Relationship*, edited by S. Hick and T. Bien. New York: Guilford.

Wittchen, H. U., M. Fuetsch, H. Sonntag, N. Müller, and M. Liebowitz. 2000. "Disability and Quality of Life in Pure and Comorbid Social Phobia: Findings from a Controlled Study." *European Psychiatry* 15(1):46–58.

Zimbardo, P. G. 1982. "Shyness and the Stresses of the Human Connection." In *Handbook of Stress: Theoretical and Clinical Aspects*, edited by L. Goldberger and S. Breznitz. New York: Free Press.

Zinbarg, R. E., D. H. Barlow, T. A. Brown, and R. M. Hertz. 1992. "Cognitive-Behavioral Approaches to the Nature and Treatment of Anxiety Disorders." *Annual Review of Psychology* 43(1):235–267.

Shannon Kolakowski, PsyD, is a licensed psychologist in private practice and the author of *When Depression Hurts Your Relationship*. Kolakowski blogs for *Huffington Post* and has appeared in media outlets such as shape.com, *Redbook*, *Men's Health* magazine, *Scientific American MIND*, and eharmony.com. She lives in Seattle, WA, with her husband. Visit the author at www.drshannonk.com.

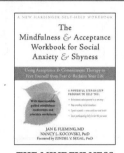
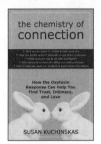

Register your **new harbinger** titles for additional benefits!

When you register your **new harbinger** title—purchased in any format, from any source—you get access to benefits like the following:

- Downloadable accessories like printable worksheets and extra content
- Instructional videos and audio files
- Information about updates, corrections, and new editions

Not every title has accessories, but we're adding new material all the time.

Access free accessories in 3 easy steps:

1. Sign in at NewHarbinger.com (or **register** to create an account).

2. Click on **register a book**. Search for your title and click the **register** button when it appears.

3. Click on the **book cover or title** to go to its details page. Click on **accessories** to view and access files.

That's all there is to it!

If you need help, visit:

NewHarbinger.com/accessories

new harbinger
CELEBRATING
40 YEARS